World War One – The Unheard Stories of Soldiers on the Western Front Battlefields

First World War stories as told by those who fought in WW1 battles – Volume One

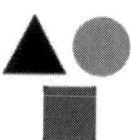

Published by Triangle Circle Square Press © 2016

All rights reserved. No text of this publication may be reproduced, distributed, or transmitted in any form or by any means, including photocopying, recording, or other electronic or mechanical methods, without the prior written permission of the publisher, except in the case of brief quotations embodied in critical reviews and certain other non-commercial uses permitted by copyright law.

This book features the work of several independent, private photographers. Where appropriate, they have been attributed for their work. Images used under any Creative Commons and GNU free license remain under their respective licenses.

"Another battery of horse gunners was dashing to the rescue."

Preface

This collection of soldier's stories relays sobering accounts of combat on the Western Front, dating to the early stages of the First World War. Evocative descriptions of the opening months of the conflict populate these pages, from which the reader can gain lessons of both the conditions of the stagnant front, and of the message the government wished to present to the public in allowing this anthology of anecdotes to be published.

A re-enactment of WW1 prisoner taking at Fort Lytton, Brisbane, Australia - Image: David Jackmanson

We see here accounts dating from the opening months of the First World War, a conflict which from our vantage point in the 21st century is synonymous with senseless carnage, catastrophic foreign policy and consequent loss of life. They are fresh recollections made weeks or months after their occurrence; their tellers not yet worn down and still committed against the enemy, whom – we are frequently reminded – has committed many atrocities, dishonouring the battlefields and war. The early humiliating loss of three naval cruisers to a single U-boat is detailed by a sailor who survived the sudden sinkings. Horses – which were to gradually disappear as the war progressed- make frequent appearances. Initial early victories, whose promise would fast diminish in the face of stagnancy on the front, also feature.

Originally released in 1915, the set of tales within this book offer a sobering account from various battlefields which took place during the early stages of the war. Although the war was not even halfway over by the time of these stories finding publication, the horrors of the war were already a fact of life, with casualties mounting rapidly on both sides.

A recreated network of WW1 trenches at the Apedale Valley Light Railway - Image: Chris Allen

The propagandists and censors of the time allowed publication of these surprisingly frank and accurate stories for two reasons: that the German enemy was duly vilified, and that the belief in the essential victory was expressed in most of the anecdotes. Despite the horrors of war, the purpose of it was alive and its soldiers were still determined and convinced of victory. Many of the storytellers were indeed, during these early stages and victories, still assured that the Germans were monstrous and their defeat impending. The short passages preluding each story often comment pointedly about the courage, bravery and cheerfulness of the teller. Compliments by the storytellers toward their commanding officers are common.

The Coltman Trench at Staffordshire Regiment Museum is a common scene for renactments - Image: WarMagician

In 1915 public opinion hadn't yet fully turned against the war, and in Britain – the nationality of all the soldiers here – the need for showing progress was essential to sustain civilian and military morale. All of the soldiers in these pages were already serving in their regiments, or had volunteered for service, when the war commenced. They were more often professional soldiers, possessed of a natural – even ingrained - patriotism, and more accepting of the official narrative than the increasingly sceptical and fearful citizenry back home. There is however no doubt that many were already disillusioned, and that the stories here are taken from an already thinning group of soldiers still possessed of some shred of belief in the war as a noble, even glorious, conflict.

Despite the mood which underpins the pages here, one can read between the lines for a picture. The stories are honest: thing got worse between those elated first weeks wherein the French welcomed their allies so gladly, and the war that was to be over by Christmas 1914 was nowhere near ending, and it is in these stories that we witness the germinal seeds of disillusion and hatred of conflict. The majority of the illustrations which originally accompanied these accounts prioritise the heroism of their subjects, while a few offer a toned down presentation of the horrific battlefields.

The modern remnants of a World War I training trench at Bodelwyddan Castle - Image: Jeff Buck

Unheard in the modern day, it is by reading between the lines of nationalist sentiment that the truth of the front emerges. It is clear that conditions rapidly worsened as the countryside was torn asunder by conflict, and that the forces of both sides were dug in with shifts in the lines increasingly rare. The implications of this – that death and carnage would carry on for a long time – gradually hit home. However it would – thanks to the efforts of Britain's censors - take longer before the rawest accounts, stripped of all nationalism, would be published.

A World War One propaganda poster from 1915

Inevitably, the truth came out, but only after the violence had claimed an enormous and notorious toll. By word of mouth rather than the popular media of the time was the grisly truth expressed - by 1916, the rate of able volunteers had fallen such that conscription was introduced. The new depths plumbed by weapons such as poisonous gas would further drive sentiment against the war. However it was only the arrival of fresh forces from the USA in 1917, together with new technologies such as the tank replacing the woefully obsolete horse, which resulted in enough breakthrough to force the end of the horrific conflict in 1918.

In this modern edition, we include a number of relevant photographic illustrations alongside the original drawings which accompanied the stories when they were first published. While the imagery of World War I is generally quite ingrained in our minds, these supplementary pictures are designed as on-the-spot reminders of how war was more than a century ago, as well as to provide demonstration of the weapons and technology of the era.

Original Introduction

By Walter Wood, 1915

All the stories in this volume are told by men who were seen personally, and who, with one or two exceptions—cases of soldiers who had returned to the front—read the typescripts of their narratives, so that accuracy should be secured. The narrators spoke while the impressions of fighting and hardships and things seen were still strong and clear; in several cases full notes had been made or diaries kept, and reference to these records was of great value in preparing the stories. When seeing an informant I specially asked that a true tale should be told, and I believe that no unreliable details were knowingly given.

I have been fortunate in getting a good deal of exclusive matter—the full record of the noble achievement of L Battery, Royal Horse Artillery, for example, has not been given anywhere in such detail as is presented here, and the same remark applies to the story of the three torpedoed cruisers.

During the earlier periods of the war British soldiers told me tales of barbarities and outrages committed by German troops which were so terrible that it was impossible to believe them, and I omitted many of these details from the finished stories; but I know now, from reading the Report of the Committee on Alleged German Outrages, presided over by Viscount Bryce, formerly British Ambassador at Washington, that even the most dreadful of the statements did not do more than touch the fringe of the appalling truth.

Though much has been already published in the form of tales and letters from our soldiers at the front, yet I hope that this collection of stories will be accepted as a contribution from the British fighting man to the general history of the earlier stages of the war—those memorable preliminary operations which have made a deep and indelible impression on the British race throughout the world.

The steam tractor 'Gigantic', which was used to pull WW1 artillery - Image: Les Chatfield

Contents

Chapter I - The Three Torpedoed Cruisers 13

Chapter II – The Runaway Raiders 25

Chapter III – Campaigning with the Highlanders 34

Chapter IV – Transport Driving............................ 44

Chapter V – British Gunners as Cave-Dwellers 52

Chapter VI – With the "Fighting Fifth"................ 63

Chapter VII - The Victory of the Marne............... 72

Chapter VII – An Armoured Car in Ambush...... 89

Chapter VIII – Exploits of the London Scottish 96

Chapter IX – The Rout of the Prussian Guard at Ypres 106

Chapter X – The British Victory at Neuve Chapelle 119

Chapter XI – Sixteen Weeks of Fighting........... 132

Chapter I - The Three Torpedoed Cruisers

Able-Seaman C. C. Nurse

[Within a few minutes, on the morning of Tuesday, September 22nd, 1914, three large British cruisers, sister ships, foundered in the North Sea, after being torpedoed by German submarines, and nearly 1,500 officers and men perished. The ships were the *Aboukir, Cressy* and *Hogue*. Each was of 12,000 tons, with a speed of twenty-two knots, and each cost £750,000. The vessels were fine warships, but almost obsolete, and before the war it had been decided to sell them out of the Navy. The *Aboukir* was torpedoed, and while the *Hogue* and *Cressy* had closed, and were standing by to save the crew, they also were torpedoed. All three ships speedily sank. The boats were filled, and, later, destroyers and other vessels came up and rescued many of the survivors, amongst whom was C. C. Nurse, an able seaman of the *Hogue*, whose story is here retold. The casualties were very heavy; but, said the Admiralty, the lives lost were "as usefully, as necessarily, and as gloriously devoted to the requirements of his Majesty's service as if the loss had been incurred in a general action."]

THE three cruisers, sister ships, were on patrol duty in the North Sea early on the morning of September 22nd. They were alone, protecting our own merchant ships and on the look-out for vessels that were mine-laying. The weather was nice, with a rather heavy swell on the water. There had been plenty of bad weather, and this was the first good day we had had for a week.

I had done my twelve years in the Navy and had been called up from the Royal Fleet Reserve. We had settled into our stride and had been in at the tail-end of the scrap in the Heligoland Bight, where the *Hogue* got hold of the *Arethusa* and towed her away. At that time the *Arethusa* had been commissioned only about two days.

We knew that she was just beginning her life; but we little thought that the *Hogue* was ending hers.

It was my watch below, and I was asleep in my hammock when the bugles sounded the *réveillé*, and we were shaken up and told that one of our ships was going down. We had turned in all standing, and lost no time in rushing on deck. Then I saw that the *Aboukir*, which was about six hundred yards away, was heeling over, and that we were steaming up to her assistance. At first we thought she had been mined; but we quickly learned that she had been torpedoed by German submarines. We were very soon alongside of her, and were doing everything we could to save the survivors. It was very clear that she was sinking, that a good many of the crew had been killed by the explosion, and that a lot of men, who were far below, in the engine-room and stokeholds, would have no chance of escaping.

We instantly started getting out the few boats that were left in our ship. There were only three, because we were cleared for action, and as it was war-time the great majority of them had been taken away. This has to be done so that there shall be as little woodwork as possible to be splintered by shells. With extraordinary speed some of the *Aboukir's* men had got to the *Hogue*, and some, who were badly hurt, had been taken to the sick-bay and were being attended to. The attack had come swiftly, and it was for us the worst of all attacks to guard against; but there was nothing like panic anywhere, and from the calmness of things you might have thought that the three ships were carrying out some ordinary evolution.

I was standing on the starboard side of the after-shelter-deck of the *Hogue*, and could see a great deal of what was going on. With remarkable smartness and speed our two lifeboats were got away to the *Aboukir*, our men pulling splendidly on their life-saving errand. Our main derrick, too, was over the side and had got the launch out. The launch was a big rowing-boat, which would hold about a hundred men, and not a second had been lost in getting her afloat under the direction of Lieutenant-Commander Clive Phillipps-Wolley.

He worked the derrick to get the launch out, though he was not in the best of health, and only a little while previously he had been ill in his bunk. He was near me on the after-bridge, which was above the shelter-deck, and I saw and heard him giving orders for the getting out of the launch. That was the last I knew about him. He was one of the lost.

The launch was afloat, and the men were ready to hurry up to the *Aboukir*; but before she could get away the very deck under my feet was blown up. There was a terrific explosion, and a huge column of wreckage rose. I was stunned for a moment by the force of the explosion. I thought we had been mined; but almost instantly there was a second explosion under me, and I knew that we had been torpedoed. The *Hogue* had been badly holed, and she began to heel over to starboard immediately.

It is only telling the plain truth to say that there was practically no confusion, and that every man was cool and going about his business as if no such thing as a calamity like this had happened. War is war, and we were ready for all sorts of things—and the discipline of the British Navy always stands firm at a crisis.

There was naturally a good deal of noise, shouting of orders, and orderly rushing to and fro as men carried them out; but everything was done with wonderful coolness, and the splendid courage of the officers was reflected in the men. A noble example was set, and it was magnificently followed. The men waited until they got their orders, just as they did at any other time.

The captain was on the fore-bridge, and I heard him shouting; but as I was so far aft I could not clearly make out what he said. I know, however, that he was ordering every man to look after himself. The men were told to take their clothes off, and to lay hands on anything that would float. They promptly obeyed, and at the word of command a lot of them jumped overboard. There was then hope that we could all get to the *Cressy*, which was still uninjured, standing by and doing all she could to rescue the survivors of her two sister ships. Soon, however, she herself was torpedoed, and in a few moments it was perfectly clear that the three ships were going to the bottom of the sea.

All the cruisers shared the same fate, and were doomed. They were the only British ships at hand, and we did not expect the enemy, being Germans, to do anything for us. But everything that skill and resource could do was done by our own survivors without a moment's loss of time. In the sea there was an amazing collection of things that had been thrown overboard—tables, chairs, spars, oars, hand-spikes, targets and furniture from the officers' cabins, such as chests of drawers. And everything that could float was badly wanted, because the sea was simply covered with men who were struggling for dear life, and knew that the fight would have to be a long and terrible one.

It takes a long time to talk of what happened, but, as a matter of fact, the whole dreadful business, so far as the loss of the ships was concerned, was over in a few minutes. As far as I can reckon, the *Hogue* herself was struck three times within a minute or so. The first torpedo came, followed almost immediately by a second in the same place, and by a third about a minute afterwards. The war-head of a torpedo holds a very big charge of gun-cotton, which, when it explodes against the side of a ship, drives an enormous hole through. An immense gap was driven in the *Hogue's* side, and there seems to be no doubt that the first torpedo struck her under the aft 9·2in. magazine. That fact would account for the fearful nature of the explosion.

As soon as the *Hogue* had been torpedoed, she began to settle by the stern; then she was quite awash aft, and began to turn turtle. Our ship sank stern first before she heeled over. There was a frightful turmoil as the four immense funnels broke away from their wire stays and went over the side, and the sea got into the stokeholds and sent up dense clouds of steam.

The Germans boast about the work having been done by one submarine, but that is nonsense. No single submarine could have done it, because she could not carry enough torpedoes. I am sure that there were at least half-a-dozen submarines in the attack; certainly when I was in the water I saw two rise. They came up right amongst the men who were swimming and struggling, and it was a curious sensation when some of the men felt the torpedoes going through the water under their legs. I did not feel that, but I did feel the terrific shock of the explosion when the first torpedo struck the *Cressy*; it came through the water towards us with very great force.

We had a fearful time in the cold water. The struggle to keep afloat and alive, the coming up of the submarines, and the rushing through the water of the torpedoes—all that we had to put up with. Then we had something infinitely worse, for the *Cressy* spotted the submarines, and instantly opened a furious fire upon them. The chief gunner, Mr. Dougherty, saw one of them as soon as her periscope appeared, and he fired, and, I believe, hit the periscope; then he fired again—and again, getting three shots in from a four-pounder within a minute, and when he had done with her, the submarine had made her last dive—and serve her right! The Germans played a dirty game on us, and only a little while before we had done our best to save some of them in the Heligoland Bight, but never a German bore a hand to save the three cruisers' men from the water. Of course, a sailor expects to be hit anyhow and anywhere in a straight piece of fighting, but this torpedoing of rescue ships was rather cold-blooded, and I don't think British submarines would have done it.

There were some awful sights—but I don't want to dwell too much on them. Men had been torn and shattered by the explosions and falling things, and there was many a broken leg and broken arm. Great numbers of men had been badly hurt and scalded inside the ship. In the engine-rooms, the stokeholds, and elsewhere, brave and splendid fellows who never left their posts had died like heroes. They never had a chance when the ships heeled over, for they were absolutely imprisoned.

When once I had reached the shelter-deck I never tried to go below again; but some of the men did, and they were almost instantly driven out by the force of the huge volumes of water which were rushing into the side through the gaping holes.

One man had an extraordinary escape. He had rushed below to get a hammock, and had laid hands on it when the ship heeled over. It seemed as if he must be drowned like a rat in a trap, and would have no chance, but the rush of water carried him along until he reached an entry-port—one of the steel doorways in the ship's sides—and then he was hurled out of the ship and into the sea, where he had, at any rate, a sporting chance, like the rest of us, of being saved.

I saw the three ships turn turtle, and a dreadful sight it was. The *Hogue* was the first to go—she was not afloat for more than seven minutes after she was struck; then the *Aboukir* went, but much more slowly—she kept afloat for rather more than half-an-hour; and the last to go was the *Cressy*. The *Cressy* heeled over very slowly and was quite a long time before she had completely turned turtle. When that happened the bottom of the ship, which was almost flat for most of its length, was where the deck had been. And on this big steel platform, which was nearly awash, the Captain was standing. I saw him quite clearly—I was not more than forty yards away—and I had seen men walking, running, crawling and climbing down the side of the ship as she heeled over. They either fell or hurled themselves into the sea and swam for it; but the captain stuck to his post to the very last and went down with his ship. It was the old British Navy way of doing things, though probably he could have saved himself if he had taken his chance in the water.

One thing which proved very useful in the water, and was the means of saving a number of lives, was a target which had been cast adrift from the *Cressy*. Targets vary in size, and this was one of the smaller ones, known as Pattern Three, about twelve feet square. It was just the woodwork without the canvas, so it floated well, and a lot of the survivors had something substantial in the way of a raft to cling to. Many of them held on gamely till the end, when rescue came; but other poor chaps dropped off from sheer exhaustion, and were drowned.

It must be remembered that not a few of the men had had an experience which was so shattering that, perhaps, there has never been anything like it in naval warfare. They were first torpedoed in the *Aboukir*, then they were taken to the *Hogue* and torpedoed in her, and then removed to the *Cressy* and torpedoed for the third time. Finally they were cast into the sea to take their chance, and, in some cases, they had to float or swim in the water for hours until they were rescued. No wonder it became a question of endurance and holding on more than a matter of swimming.

The sea was covered with men who were either struggling for life or holding on to wreckage. The boats were packed, and well they might be, because no effort had been spared to get struggling men into them. The men who were in the best of health and good swimmers were helping those who could not swim, and in this way many a man was saved who would have been lost.

When I was in the water I did not utter a word to anybody—it was not worth it, and you needed all your breath; but I never abandoned hope, even when I saw the last ship go down, because I knew that we should have assistance.

Wireless calls were made, and appeals for help were being sent out all the time, and when I looked around at all, it was in the hope of seeing some of our own ships tearing down to the rescue. My mind was easy on the point—I knew that the call must have been made, and it was merely a question of time for the response to come.

I was supported by a plank and clung to it with all my strength, though from time to time I endured agony from cramp. In spite of the torture I never let go. I gripped my plank, but I saw men near me forced to let go their hold of things they had seized, and they were drowned. In many cases cramp overcame them, and quite near to me were poor fellows who were so contracted with it that they were doubled up in the water, with their knees under their chins. I could see their drawn faces and knotted hands—and in several cases I saw that the grip which was on the floating objects was the grip of death. I floated past these poor chaps, and it was pitiful to see them. Thank God some of the struggling in the water did not last long, because many of the men had been badly burnt or scalded, or hit by heavy pieces of wreckage, and these soon fell away exhausted, and were drowned. Some, too, were dazed and lost their nerve as well as their strength, so that they could not keep up the fight for life. For long after the cruisers had sunk, carrying hundreds of men with them, the sea for a great space was covered with floating bodies—dead sailors, as well as those who had managed to live.

Whenever a boat came up I tried to help a man into it; but it was not possible to do anything except with the aid of the boats. The two cutters acted splendidly, picking up all the men they could. Captain Nicholson, of the *Hogue*, was in charge of one of them, and he did some rousing rescue work.

There were some fine deeds of courage and unselfishness that sad morning in the North Sea. The launch and the cutter were packed, of course, and seeing this, and knowing that there were men in the water who were more badly wanting a place in the boat than he was, a Royal Fleet Reserve man, named Farmstone, sprang into the sea and swam for it, to make room for a man who was exhausted.

I was thankful indeed when I saw smoke on the horizon—black clouds which showed that some ships were steaming up as hard as they could lick. Very soon, some of our own destroyers—blessed and welcome sight—came into view, and as they did so, I believe, they potted at submarines which were slinking away, but I can't say with what result. The destroyers came up. The *Lucifer*, a small cruiser, came up too, and the work of rescue began as hard as it could be carried out, every officer and man working with a will. There were two or three other ships about, two Lowestoft trawlers—which did uncommonly good work—and two small Dutch steamers, one called the *Titan* and the other the *Flora*. The next thing that I clearly remember was that I had been hauled out of the bitter-cold water and lifted on board the *Flora*, and that she was soon packed with half-dead men like myself.

The *Flora* was a very small Dutch cargo boat, and with so many men on board she was crammed. It is impossible to say how some of the men got on board, and they could not explain themselves, they were so utterly exhausted. The Dutch could understand us, though words were hardly necessary, and they shared everything they had—clothes, food, drink and accommodation. They wrapped their bedding round us and gave us hot coffee. The stokehold was crowded with men who had gone down into it to get dry and warm. Some of the men were suffering dreadfully from burns, wounds and exhaustion, and one of them died on board the *Flora*. He was my next messmate, Green. He lived for only about an hour. I saw him in one of the seamen's bunks, and he was then in great agony. I think he had been struck very badly in the explosion. We took him away from the bunk, laid him on the fore-hatch and covered him with a tarpaulin, where he lay till about five o'clock in the afternoon, when we landed at Ymuiden. Poor Green was buried there with full honours, the British chaplain at Amsterdam conducting the service.

One very strange incident of the disaster was the way in which the ensign of the *Hogue* was saved. I don't know how it happened, but one of the stokers who had managed to escape got hold of the ensign when he was in the water, and hung on to it all the time he was in—two or three hours. He had the ensign with him when we were in Holland, and had his photograph taken with it in the background.

Another remarkable fact is that four brothers, who came from the Yorkshire coast, I think, were in the *Hogue*, and all of them were saved!

Talking of photographs, I was one of a group which was taken at Ymuiden, when we were rigged out in the kit of Dutch bluejackets. There I am, in the back row. At that time I was wearing a beard and moustache, as there was neither much time not inclination for shaving.

We had lost everything we had, and were almost naked, so we were very glad of the clothes that were given to us by the Dutch. These people were kindness itself to us, and did everything they could to make us comfortable and happy. I was taken to a small café and went to bed.

A Dutch soldier was in charge of us, but he had no fear of us doing any harm. Next evening they took us by train to a place in the north of Holland; then we had a sixteen miles' tramp along the level roads to a concentration camp where there were some Belgian prisoners, who gave us a cheer.

"Good swimmers were helping those who could not swim."

We marched those sixteen miles whistling and singing. Had we not been snatched from death?

We had to rough it, of course, but that came easy after such an experience as ours. There was only one blanket amongst thirteen men, and we had to sleep on straw, and eat with our fingers. We had plenty of food, though—rough, but very nice, and we were very glad of it, and thankful to get a drink of water.

Next morning, when we left the straw and solitary blanket, it was very raw and cheerless, and there was a heavy mist. The Belgian prisoners had a football, and we borrowed it and played a game, and got warm. We were covered with straw, and our clothes were filled with it when we woke, but we soon shook it clear when we got going with the ball. We enjoyed a basin of coffee and a big lump of brown bread which the Dutch cook gave us, then we got the time on by turning our tents out, and were quite in clover when the British Consul supplied us with knives, forks, spoons, towels, overcoats and boots.

We spent the first morning washing and drying our socks, and wondering what was going to be done with us. We kept on wondering, but soon knew that we were not going to be detained in Holland, but were to be sent home. On the Friday we had definite news that we were to go back to England, and on the Saturday morning we left, and did the sixteen miles' tramp again; but it was easier this time, because we were prepared for it. We stopped at a farm, and they gave us milk and food, cigars and cigarettes, and before entering a special train for Flushing, the Dutch gave us milk again, and cake, bread and apples.

From Flushing we came on to Sheerness, and then we went on leave—and here I am; but I go back in a day or two. I don't know what will happen, for owing to the explosion the sight of my left eye has practically gone. Besides that, I seem to have been completely shattered in nerves, though I reckoned that I was one of those men who have no nerves—I have been a steeple-jack since I left the Navy, and just before I was called up I was cleaning the face of Big Ben.

It is when I wake in the middle of the night, as I often do, that the whole fearful thing comes back with such awful vividness, and I see again the dreadful sights that it is better to forget.

Yes, the Germans got three good hauls in the cruisers; but I don't think they'll have another chance like it.

A U Boat sinks an Allied ship during World War One - Painting by Willy Stower

HMS Aboukir - one of the three ships sunk by a single U Boat on 22 September 1914

Chapter II – The Runaway Raiders

Sapper W. Hall, Royal Engineers

["Practically the whole fast cruiser force of the German Navy, including some great ships vital to their fleet and utterly irreplaceable, has been risked for the passing pleasure of killing as many English people as possible, irrespective of sex, age or condition, in the limited time available. Whatever feats of arms the German Navy may hereafter perform, the stigma of the baby-killers of Scarborough will brand its officers and men while sailors sail the seas." So wrote the First Lord of the Admiralty (Mr. Winston S. Churchill) on December 20th, 1914, in reference to the German raid on Scarborough, Whitby, and the Hartlepools on December 16th. In that cowardly bombardment of unprotected places, the Huns killed more than a hundred men, women, and children in the Hartlepools alone, and altogether the casualties numbered more than six hundred. This story is based on the narrative of Sapper W. Hall, R.E., one of the few English soldiers who have been under an enemy's fire on English soil. Sapper Hall was badly wounded.]

IT is just a fortnight to-day since the German warships came up out of the mist, bombarded Hartlepool, wrecked many of the houses, killed a lot of defenceless women, children and men, and then tore away into the mist as hard as they could steam. Our own warships nearly got up with them, and if it had not been for the mist, never one of those vessels which were so valiant in bombarding helpless towns would have got back to Germany.

A great deal of confusion has been caused in telling the story of the raids on the Hartlepools, the two places being hopelessly mixed up. They are, as a matter of fact, quite separate towns, with separate mayors and corporations.

Hartlepool itself, where we now are, is on the coast, facing the sea; West Hartlepool is two miles inland. Both towns were bombarded, but it is hereabouts that most of the damage by shells was done, and many children and grown-up people killed. It was just over there, too, that eight Territorials were standing on the front, watching the firing, when a shell struck them and killed seven of the men and wounded the eighth.

It was soon after eight o'clock in the morning when we rushed out of our billets into the streets, and, looking seaward, we saw warships firing.

In our billets we had heard the booming of guns, and supposing that it was our own warships practising or fighting, we had hurried out to see the fun. A few seconds was enough to tell us that there was no fun in it, but that this was a bombardment in deadly earnest by the enemy.

The German ships were easily visible from the shore, and did not seem to be very far away—about two miles. They were firing rapidly, and there was a deafening noise as the shells screamed and burst—the crashing of the explosions, the smashing of immense numbers of window-panes by the concussion, and the thudding of the shells and fragments against walls and buildings.

Coming so unexpectedly, the bombardment caused intense excitement and commotion, and men, women and children rushed into the streets to see what was happening—the worst thing they could do, because the splinters of shell, horrible jagged fragments, were flying all about and killing and maiming the people they struck. A number of little children who had rushed into the streets, as children will, were killed or wounded.

As soon as we realised what was happening, we rushed back and got our rifles and hurried into the street again, and did what we could; but rifles were absolutely useless against warships, and the incessant bursting of shells and the scattering of fragments and bullets made it most dangerous to be in the open.

Shells were striking and bursting everywhere, wrecking houses, ploughing into the ground, and battering the concrete front of the promenade.

The houses hereabouts, overlooking the sea, were big and easy targets for the Germans, who blazed away like madmen, though they must have been in terror all the time when they thought that their cannonading was sure to fetch British warships up. How thankful they must have felt for that protecting mist!

The Hartlepool Rovers' Football Ground is very near the sea and the lighthouse, and it came under heavy fire. One of our men, Sapper Liddle, was near the wall of the ground when a shell burst and mortally wounded him, injuring him terribly. It was not possible to get at him and bring him into hospital for a long time, but when he was brought here everything that was humanly possible was done for him. He lingered for a few hours, then died.

Meanwhile, death and destruction were being dealt out all around us, and the land batteries were making such reply as they could to the Germans' heavy guns. This reply was a very plucky performance, for Hartlepool is not a fortified place in anything like the real meaning of the word, and our light guns were no match for the weapons of the German battle-cruisers.

As it happened, no damage was done to the guns; but fearful mischief was caused to buildings near us. A shell struck the Baptist Chapel fair and square on the front, and drove a hole in it big enough for the passage of a horse and cart; then it wrecked the inside and went out at the other end of the chapel, again making a huge hole.

House after house was struck and shattered, in some cases people being buried in the ruins. Some of the houses are very old, and pretty well collapsed when a shell struck them and burst.

While the bombardment was in progress we were doing our best, but that could not be much. There was not much cause for laughter, but I remember that a shell came and burst near us, and made us see the humour of a little incident. The explosion itself did no actual damage, but the concussion and force of it were so violent that a sapper was jerked up into the air and came down with a crash. He picked himself up and scuttled as hard as he could make for shelter.

The firing was so sudden and so fierce that it was begun and finished almost before it was possible to realise that it had taken place. Most of the men of Hartlepool were at work when the bombardment started, and some of them were killed at their work, or as they were rushing home to see to their wives and children, while some were killed as they fled for safety.

The streets were crowded with fugitives during the bombardment, and it was owing to this that so many people were killed and wounded. The shells burst among them with awful results.

While the Germans were firing point-blank at the buildings facing the sea, and deliberately killing inoffensive people, they were also bombarding West Hartlepool, and doing their best to blow up the gasworks, destroy the big shipbuilding yards there, and set fire to the immense stacks of timber which are stored in the yards.

People were killed who were five or six miles from the guns of the warships, and in one street alone in West Hartlepool seven persons, mostly women, were killed. Several babies were killed in their homes, and little children were killed as they played in the streets.

A good deal has been said about the number of shells that were fired from the German warships, and some people had put down a pretty low total; but from what I saw, I should think that certainly five hundred shells of all sorts were fired by these valiant Germans, who knew that they were perfectly safe so far as the shore was concerned, and took mighty good care not to be caught by British ships of their own size and power; but that will surely come later, and the men of the North will get their own back.

I cannot say anything about the actual defences, or what the military did; but the few troops who were here did their best, and a couple of destroyers bore a brave part in the affair.

A shell fell in the lines of the Royal Engineers, and several dropped in the lines of the 18th Service Battalion of the Durham Light Infantry.

It was very quickly known, as I have mentioned, that seven out of eight men of the Durhams, who were watching the firing—thinking, like everybody else, that it was some sort of battle practice, till they learned the real truth—had been killed by the explosion of a shell, and that the eighth man had been wounded; but there were several other cases of men being wounded which were not known about until later, because of the great difficulties of discovering the men amongst the ruins which the shell-fire had caused.

From the moment the bombardment began there was an awful commotion, and the noise grew until it was simply deafening. The whole town literally shook, and while the firing lasted there was a tremendous and continuous vibration—everything shivered and rattled. One shell struck the wall of the football ground, which faces the sea; not far away a hole was dug in the ground by one of the very first of the shells that were fired; the fine old church of St. Hilda was damaged, and the side of the rectory was simply peppered by a bursting shell.

In the particular place where I and my chums were, the shells were coming in a shower, and doing enormous mischief. We could see that plainly enough. But it was not until later, when the German warships had steamed away as hard as they could go, that we knew how great the damage had been, and how many lives had been lost and people wounded.

The German ships fired from one side to begin with, then they turned round and continued the bombardment from the other side, so they must have been ready loaded all round. The size of the shots varied from the 12-inch shells, perfect monsters, to the small ones which came so fast and did so much havoc. The fact that some of the huge shells were found unexploded after the bombardment proves that ships of great size took part in the raid.

Some time after the firing began I felt a blow on my thigh, and fell to the ground, helpless, though I did not know at the time what had happened. At last, when the firing—which continued for about forty minutes—ceased, stretcher-bearers and volunteer ambulance workers set about collecting the wounded, and I was picked up and brought to the hospital here.

It was then found that I had been struck on the thigh by part of the cap of a shell, and that I had sustained a compound fracture. The piece of metal was still sticking in me—you can see it later. It was taken out, and I was promptly and most kindly looked after, as were all our men who had been wounded and were brought in. Poor Liddle, as I have told you, was not discovered for some time; then he was found and brought here, and died late at night, in spite of all the efforts that were made to save him. He had a real soldier's funeral—just as had the rest of the soldiers who had been killed.

WW1 Commonwealth soldier graves at Ypres Reservoir cemetary - Image: Redvers

"The 'Hogue' began to turn turtle. The four immense funnels broke away."

As soon as the bombardment was over the people set to work to collect the dead as well as save the wounded, and both were heavy tasks; but there were many willing hands. Even in half-an-hour a wonderful difference had been made in the streets, and those people who had been rushing towards the country for safety began to return. They brought in reports of losses which had been suffered in the outskirts through shells; but, as I have said, the worst cases of all were just about here.

One house was completely demolished, and the father, mother, and half-a-dozen children were killed, so that home and family were wiped out in an instant. One part of the Old Town is so utterly destroyed that it is called "Louvain," and if you look at the houses there you will find that they are just heaps of rubbish and ruins, with beds and furniture and so on, buried.

Shells had exploded in the streets, in houses, fields, at the gasworks, in shipyards—anywhere and everywhere—and one big thing stuck itself in a house and is kept as a relic. Another crashed through four railway waggons, and another shell, which travelled low on the ground, went through several sets of the steel metals on the railway, which shows the fearful penetrative power of the projectile.

If the Germans had had their way, no doubt this place would have been wiped out altogether. They made a dead set at the gasworks, but did not do a great deal of mischief there, though it meant that that night a lot of people had to burn candles instead of gas. And though more than a hundred people were killed, and the Germans fondly supposed that they had struck terror into the place, they had done nothing of the sort.

The residents were soon clearing up the ruins and settling down again as if nothing had happened. The most pitiful of all the tasks was that of dealing with the dead and wounded children, and the remembrance of the sad sights will be the best of all inspirations for some of our fellows when the day comes on which they will get their own back from the Germans.

It was not long before we learned that at about the same time as we were being shelled at Hartlepool, German warships had appeared off the entirely undefended places of Whitby and Scarborough. They call these old fishing ports fortified, but that is an absolute untruth, and they know it. But the Germans were out to kill and destroy, and they did both in a manner which showed that they had made calculations to a minute, and that their spies had been long at work.

At Scarborough the raiders did a lot of damage before they ran away. They had prepared one of their boasted surprises for us, and we got it; but that was nothing to the surprise we gave them on Christmas morning at Cuxhaven—a real fortified place—and nothing, I hope and believe, to the surprises that our Navy has in store for the German naval runaways.

You ask how long shall I be in hospital.

That is hard to tell; but I have been here two weeks already, and I suppose that I shall be here for at least six weeks longer.

I keep the piece of shell which struck me, in a bit of brown paper in the cupboard near the head of the bed. I cannot rise to get it myself, but if you will open the little door you will find it. It's the sort of thing which caused such havoc in the Hartlepools when the German warships came and bombarded us.

A cross section of World War One era shells - Image: Historiclair

Chapter III – Campaigning with the Highlanders

Private A. Veness, 2nd Battalion Seaforth Highlanders.

[The Highland regiments have made a great impression upon the Germans since the war began, and the kilted troops have added to their laurels in the field. This story of fighting with the Highlanders is told by Private A. Veness, 2nd Battalion Seaforth Highlanders, who was wounded and invalided home.]

I HAVE served eight years in the Seaforth Highlanders. To begin with I was a bandsman, but when the war broke out and I was recalled to the colours, I became an ordinary private, and the only music that the Germans heard me play was the rattle of my rifle. When we landed in France and marched off to the front the girls seemed to have a special fancy for the kilted men—at any rate they crowded up and hugged and kissed those they could get hold of; so we went off in very good spirits, singing and whistling popular tunes, not forgetting the Marseillaise and "Tipperary."

Being a strange country we saw a good many things that were new and very strange to us till we got used to them. One amusing incident happened as soon as we were in Belgium, and that was the sight of a big fat man being pulled in a little cart by two dogs. It was funny, but still it made us angry, for we rather looked upon it as cruelty to animals; so we shouted, "Lazy brute!" "Get out and give the dogs a ride!" and so on, and I daresay the man was greatly surprised, though he didn't know what we were saying. In a little while we understood that dogs are extensively used for haulage purposes in Belgium and we ceased to take any special notice of them.

It was not long after landing before we were told to be ready for the Germans, but that proved a false alarm. We were, however, to get our baptism of fire in a dramatic fashion, and that baptism naturally dwells in my mind more vividly than many of the far bigger things which happened later in the war.

A terrific thunderstorm broke, and a party of us were ordered to billet in a barn. We climbed up into a loft and began to make ourselves comfortable and to make some tea. We had scarcely got the welcome tea to our lips when the hurried order came to clear out of the building, and into the thunderstorm we dashed. Then the German shells began to fly and burst, and in a few minutes the barn was struck and shattered, so that we had a very narrow escape.

It was at this stage that we had our first man killed. He was a chum of mine, a bandsman, named Dougal McKinnon. While we were having our tea Dougal was under cover in the trenches, in front of the barn, with his company. They were under shell fire, and he was killed by bursting shrapnel. He was buried close to the spot where he fell, and being the first of our men to be killed in action we felt it very deeply. Many times after that, when our chums were killed, we had to leave them, because we had no time to bury them.

We got on the move, and when night came it was awful to see the whole countryside lit up with the flames of burning buildings—farms and houses and other places which had been set on fire by the Germans. There was a farm which was blazing furiously and I shall never forget it, for the good reason that in marching we managed to circle it three times before we could get properly on the march and go ahead.

We pushed on to Cambrai, where the cannonading was truly terrible. My company was in support of another company in advance. We lay behind a bank, sheltering, for a few hours. At the back of us was a British howitzer battery, in a bit of a wood, so that we were between two awful fires. It was indescribable—the deafening din, which never ceased or lessened while the duel raged, the excitement, the danger, and the nerve-strain; yet there was something fascinating in watching the firing and wondering what was going to happen.

It is wonderful to think of the working of the human mind at such a time, and strange to recall the odd things one does. In our own case, as we had to go on sheltering and watching, we amused ourselves by counting the number of shells that dropped within a certain area which was well under our observation. The area was, roughly speaking, about 200 yards square, and in three-quarters of an hour no fewer than seventy-six shells exploded over that particular spot. They were shrapnel and high explosive and never struck the ground—they burst in the air, and at one time I counted six shells bursting in the air together. That gives you some idea of the tremendous nature of the German shell fire. Luckily a great number of the shells did not explode at all, or few if any of us could have got away.

It is impossible to praise too highly the British artillery's work. To my own personal knowledge there was one battery that day—I don't know which it was—which was under fire for at least seven hours continuously without shifting; and during the whole of that time they were replying to the German guns.

After that shattering experience we camped in a cornfield at night, and were settling down to sleep when were we ordered to move again. For hours, worn and weary though we were, we were on the march, and thankful we were when we halted in a village and got a box of biscuits from the French as a midday snack. We had been forced to part with most of our equipment and many of the greatcoats were thrown away; but I felt that I should want mine and I stuck to it—and I am wearing it now. It has had plenty of rough usage—and here are the holes made by a piece of flying shrapnel.

I am proud to say that the general in command of our division congratulated the regiment on its splendid marching, and I think we did a fine thing, for in about twelve hours we covered about thirty-two miles—actual marching, with just a halt here and there. The Germans had done their best to trap us, but they had not succeeded, and we escaped, to turn the tables on them with a vengeance.

That night I had to report sick—there was something wrong with my ankles. I was unable to march, so I got a lift on a limber-waggon of the 88th Battery of the Royal Field Artillery. During the ride, which lasted all night, I went through some of the finest country I ever saw. It was particularly beautiful because of the time of the year, late autumn, and the clear light of the full moon. This moonlight ride on a limber will be always associated in my memory with the grandest spectacle of its sort I saw during the war.

The battery was travelling along a switchback road, and I was wrapped up in the beautiful and peaceful scenery—it was hard to believe that this calm landscape was the scene of war and that the splendid British gunners I was with had been dealing death and destruction amongst the Germans so lately.

Not far away was a river, winding like a silver thread over the face of the country, and suddenly, from the river, there rose an immense mass of flame and smoke, followed quickly by a thunderous rumbling roar.

I knew at once that a bridge had been blown up. I cannot tell you who destroyed it—Germans or French; all I know is that I saw the sight and it was the most remarkable of its kind that I witnessed—and I saw four splendid bridges destroyed in this manner.

At one time we had crossed a fine bridge and as soon as we had done so a hole was dug and a mine was laid in the centre. Then our cyclist section was sent out to report what was going to happen and the bridge was blown up. In this case we were the last to cross before the explosion occurred.

At an early stage of the operations I was lucky enough to see a very fine fight in the air, a duel between a French airman and a German airman. I was able to follow the duel for miles. The men in the aeroplanes were firing revolvers at each other and we could hear the crack of the shots, though we could not see any definite results, because the duel got too far away. This was the first fight in the air that I saw, and I watched it with extraordinary interest, especially as we all keenly hoped that the German would be brought down, because he had been flying over our lines and quickly directed shell fire on us owing to his signals. For fully twenty minutes I watched this air fight. It was wonderful to see the swiftness with which the machines dived and dodged. The Frenchman circled over the German in the most skilful and daring manner and time after time threatened his existence.

Another remarkable incident I witnessed at this time was the escape of a German cavalryman. He was an Uhlan, a scout, I take it, and quite alone. We were on the march and had been told that the German cavalry were in large numbers near us, and so that we should be ready for them we took up a position, with some Irish infantry to the left of us.

We were lying in position on a hill, and in front of us was three or four miles of good flat country, so that we should have had a fine view of cavalry in force. We watched and waited, but the threatened cavalry did not come—all we saw was this solitary Uhlan, a mere speck on the wide plain.

As soon as the Uhlan was seen the rifles rattled and it was expected that he would be potted; but he seemed to bear a charmed life. The Irish battalion gave him a particularly heavy fire—the Seaforths were too far off to reach him with the rifle; but the Uhlan galloped gaily on, and it was quite amusing to watch him. No doubt he thoroughly enjoyed himself—at any rate he galloped unscathed across two or three miles of open country, and got away.

It was not until we were within about eighteen miles of Paris that the retirement ended and we began the offensive. We had had a very hard time, and were to have a few days' rest, but we never got it. Yet in spite of the hardships we had some very pleasant times, because of the beauty of the country and the season.

Joyful indeed was the day when we began to drive the Germans back, and it was the more joyful because the advance was almost as swift as our retirement had been.

On that wonderful advance we saw some horrible things—I will not dwell on German barbarities, though there were many proofs of them—including great numbers of horses which had been killed or wounded and left just where they had fallen. No attempt had been made to dispose of the decaying carcases and many a poor brute had died a lingering death.

I was greatly struck by the Germans' cruelty to their horses, in leaving them like this; but that was one proof of the hurriedness of the enemy's retreat—the Germans who had got so near Paris and were then flung right away back from the city. I need hardly say that whenever a sign of movement was noticed in a horse a man was sent to put the poor thing out of its misery.

There was still plenty of hardship to put up with, but that did not matter so much when we were driving back the Germans.

I remember very well one day and night of uncommon wretchedness. It was raining heavily and continuously, and in the deluge I and three more men were sent on outpost—to observe and keep our eyes open, and so that we could do that to the best advantage we took up a position on the top of a hayrick. A perfect hurricane was blowing, and the almost solid rain was fairly driven into us; but we stuck it through, and hung on to the top of the haystack till it was dark, then we thankfully got down and went into an open shed for shelter—a building that was just a protection for wheat-stacks.

I had had my turn of picketing and was lying down to get a snatch of sleep when I was ordered to go up a road about a mile and a half away, to find out whether our relief had come. So out into the darkness and the wind and rain I staggered and fought my way through what was the worst night for weather that I ever saw. On and on I and my comrades went, looking hard for our relief, but we never saw it, and we waited there till next morning, when we rejoined our brigade.

Those were times when there was little rest for the Seaforths, or anybody else.

The aeroplanes gave us little chance of rest, and at times they had an uncanny knack of finding us.

One day, after a long, hard march, we put into a wood for shelter. A French supply column was already in the wood and doubtless the Germans knew of or suspected this; at any rate a German aeroplane came over us, with the result that in a few minutes we were shelled out. We rested in another part of the wood till it was dark, then we were taken on to billets, but we had to make another move, because we were shelled out again. That was the sort of thing which came along as part of the day's work; and as part of the day's work we took it cheerfully.

When we got the Germans on the move we took prisoners from time to time. I was on guard over a few prisoners, part of a crowd, when one of them came up to me and to my amazement I recognised him as a German who had worked in Soho Square and used often to go to the same place as myself for dinner—a little shop in Hanway Street, at the Oxford Street end of Tottenham Court Road. The prisoner recognised me at once and I recognised him. To show how ignorant the Germans were of the enemy they were fighting, I may tell you that this man said to me, "If we had known we were fighting the English, I would never have left London!"

Was it not strange that the two of us, who had so often met as friends for dinner in the little foreign shop, should meet again as enemies on the banks of the Marne?

I am now coming to a sorrowful personal incident—the loss of my chum, Lance-Corporal Lamont. We had been together from the beginning of the war and had shared everything there was, even to the waterproof sheet. He would carry the sheet one day and I would carry it the next, and whenever such a thing had to be done as fetching drinking-water, often a very dangerous task, we would share that too.

Throughout one awful night of ceaseless rain, which soaked us to the skin, the two of us were in the trenches—we had dug ourselves in, with just ordinary head cover. We lay there till next morning, when an officer came along my platoon and asked if we had any drinking-water.

We told him that we had not.

The officer said, "If you care to risk it, one of you can go and fetch some water."

We decided to take the risk, which was great, because to get the water meant getting to a farmhouse just behind us, under a heavy fire.

My chum volunteered to go, and, taking the water-bottles, he left the trench and started to cross the open ground between us and the farmhouse. While he was doing this the order came for us to advance—and I never saw him again.

It was soon my turn to be put out of action. A pretty stiff fight was going on and the fire was so heavy that it was very dangerous to be in the open; but it was necessary for me and a few more men to cross a bit of open ground, and we made a start. We had not gone far when a shell came between me and another man who was at my side. The shell struck him fair on the arm and shattered it. He fell over on his side, and as he did so he said, "For Heaven's sake cut my equipment off!"

I took out my jack-knife and slit the equipment across the shoulders and let it drop away from him.

He crawled off and I was told afterwards that while he was trying to creep to shelter he was struck again and killed.

I crawled as best I could up to the firing line, but when I got there I found that there was no room in the trenches for me, so I had to lie in the open. I had not been there long before a fellow next to me asked me what time it was. I took out my watch and told him it was about eleven-fifteen—and the next thing I knew was that I felt as if someone had kicked me on the top of the head.

I turned round and said, "Tommy, I'm hit!" I became unconscious for some time, then, when I recovered, I said, "Tommy, is it safe to crawl away?"

"No," said Tommy, "it's risky. It's a bit too hot!"

"Never mind," I answered. "If I stay here much longer I shall collapse. I'm going to have a shot at it—here goes!"

I began to crawl away, but I must have taken the wrong direction, for I was soon under two fires. I was approaching the mouths of two or three of our own guns, which were in front of a farmhouse.

I soon found that this was a bit too warm for me, and so I turned and took what I supposed was the right direction. I had had enough of crawling, which was very slow work. I wanted to get out of it, and I made up my mind to rise and run. That does not sound very brave, but it was the better part of valour.

I started to run, as best I could; but I had hardly got going when a bullet struck me, as I supposed, and I collapsed alongside some of my own comrades.

Stretcher-bearers came up, in time, and I was carried to the field hospital. Then a curious discovery was made, which was, that a bullet had gone through four or five pleats of my kilt and had stuck in my leg, high up. This is the place where it struck and stuck and here's the bullet, which the doctor easily pulled out with his fingers, for it had not penetrated deeply, owing, I think, to the resistance of the pleats of my kilt. Apart from this bullet wound I was struck by shrapnel four times, but I managed to keep going.

I left the field hospital the next day and joined an ambulance column which was shelled by the Germans as it went along. I escaped myself, but one of the waggons was completely wrecked.

Having recovered from my wound to a certain extent I went back to the regiment, but after a few days I had to be invalided home, and I have had a long and tedious spell in hospital.

There is one more incident I would like to mention by way of closing. We halted in a village in France where we saw some of the Turcos, one of whom was very noticeable because he was proudly wearing the greatcoat of a German officer which he had secured on the battlefield, after killing the officer.

While we halted, a batch of German prisoners was brought into the village, and they were put into a courtyard between two rows of cottages. No sooner had this been done than an old man rushed out, and if it had not been for the guard he would have hurled himself upon the prisoners and done his best to thrash them.

The act was so strange that I inquired the reason for the old man's fury. And the answer I received was, "He remembers 1870."

"A bullet struck him in the back and killed him."

Chapter IV – Transport Driving

Private James Roache, Army Service Corps.

[It was estimated that, early in the war, no fewer than 10,000 vehicle workers were serving with the colours—3000 taxicab drivers, 3000 tramway men, and 4000 motor-'bus drivers. These trained men went from London and the provinces, some being Reservists, and others joining various regiments; but a very large number went into the Transport Section, and did splendid work. From this story by Private James Roache, Mechanical Transport Section, Siege Artillery Brigade, we learn something of the heavy and perilous work that falls to the lot of the Transport Section, and can realise the enormous extent to which the Army depends upon its transport.]

I GOT into Ypres about seven days after the Germans had left the city, and I learned from a school-teacher who spoke English that they had commandeered a good many things, and had pillaged the jewellers' shops and other places of business.

At that time the Germans did not seem to have done any exceptional damage; but they made up for any neglect later on, when they acted like barbarians in bombarding and destroying the beautiful old city, and smashing its priceless ancient buildings into ruins. That is part of the system of savagery which they boast about as "culture."

We had been in Ypres about a week when the first German shell came. It was the beginning of a fearful havoc. That was about ten o'clock in the morning. The shell dropped plumb into the prison. There were a good many civil prisoners in the gaol at the time, but I do not know what happened to them, and I cannot say whether any of the helpless creatures were killed or wounded.

At that time I was helping to supply the Siege Artillery Brigade, the guns of which—the famous 6 in. howitzers—were a mile or so out of the city. We had four cars, each carrying three tons of lyddite—twelve tons in all—standing in the Market Square, and exposed to the full artillery fire of the enemy.

It was a perilous position, for if a shell had struck that enormous amount of lyddite probably the whole city would have been wrecked, and the loss of life would have been appalling. We had to wait for several hours before we could move, because of the difficulty in communicating with the brigade; but when the order did at last arrive, we lost no time in getting to a safer place than the Market Square.

It was while we were standing under fire that I saw a mother and her child—a girl—struck by a fragment of a bursting shell. They were the first people to be wounded in Ypres.

The shell—a big brute—burst on the roof of a house, and the fragments scattered with terrific force all around. People were flying for their lives, or hiding, terror-stricken, in the cellars; and the woman and her daughter were struck as we watched them fly.

Some of us rushed up and found that one of the boots of the woman had been ripped open, and that the child had been struck on the face and badly cut.

I picked her up, and saw that she was unconscious; but I got at my field-dressing and did all I could for her, and was thankful to find that she soon came back to her senses, though she was suffering terribly from shock and began to cry bitterly.

The mother also was dreadfully upset, but not seriously hurt. We lost no time in getting them into the underground part of a café near at hand, and there we had to leave them. I don't know what became of them, but I suppose they were taken away. I often wonder what has happened to the poor little soul and her mother, victims, like so many thousands more, of the German invaders. I am glad to know that with our field-dressings we were able to help a good many civilians who were wounded.

The four cars I have mentioned were big transport-lorries, made specially for the war, and very fine work can be done with them. But how different the work is from that which we used to do at home as motor-drivers!—and I had a fair experience of that before I joined the Transport Service. There was as much difference between the two as there is between this war and the South African War, in which I served in the Imperial Yeomanry.

These lorries carried immense quantities of ammunition, and so the Germans made a special point of going for them, in the hope of bringing about a destructive explosion; but, taken on the whole, they had very poor luck that way.

When the order came to us in the Market Square at Ypres to march, we left the city and travelled along the roads till it was dark; and after that we returned to the city, taking the stuff with us. No sooner were we back in Ypres than the Germans started shelling again, after having ceased fire for about four hours.

What we carried was wanted for the guns, but we could not reach them, owing to the excessive danger from the German fire. It is a strange fact that as soon as any stuff was going through by transport the Germans started shelling it, which seems to show that they had word when transports were on the move. They shelled us constantly, and we got to take the thing as a very ordinary part of the day's work.

It was only when some uncommon explosion occurred that we were roused to take notice; and such an event took place one day when one of the very biggest of the German shells burst in the air not far away from me with a tremendous crash, and made an immense cloud of awful smoke and rubbish as the fragments struck the ground.

This explosion was so near and so unusual that I thought I would get hold of a souvenir of it. And so I did. I secured a piece of the base of the shell, and meant to bring it home as a trophy; but I had to leave it, for the weight of the fragment was 95 lb., and that's a trifle heavy even for a transport-driver. This was certainly one of the very biggest and most awful of the German shells of the immense number I saw explode.

There is, or was, a skittle-alley in Ypres, near the water-tower, and some of the Munsters were billeted there. I was near the place when some very heavy shelling was going on, and I saw one shell burst on the building with a terrific report. I knew at once that serious damage was done, and that there must have been a heavy loss of life, for I saw wounded and unwounded men rushing into the street from the ruined building. Some of the men were bandaging themselves as they rushed out. I knew that there must be a shocking sight inside the building; so when the commanding officer said, "Would you like to go inside and look at it?" I replied that I would rather not. And I was glad afterwards, for I learned that six poor fellows had been killed. That was the sort of thing which was constantly happening to our fighting men, and it was bad enough; but it was infinitely worse when the victims were women and children, as they so often were, and it was the sight of these innocent sufferers which was the hardest of all to bear. Some of our youngsters were particularly upset.

There was a little trumpeter of the Royal Garrison Artillery, to which we were attached, and a fine youngster he was, about sixteen years old. We called him "Baggie." He used to stick it very well, but at times, when he saw women and children hurt, he gave way and cried. But that kind-heartedness did not prevent him from being always eager to come with us when we took the ammunition up to the guns in the firing line. "Baggie" never knew fear for himself, but he felt it badly when others were hit or hurt, and that took place day after day.

There was another little trumpeter of the Royal Engineers who got badly upset for the same reason. He was billeted in a timber-yard, and I saw a shell fall in the yard and burst and send the timber flying in all directions. It seemed as if tremendous mischief had been done, and that there must have been a heavy loss of life; but, as a matter of fact, only one man was injured on the head and face by splinters.

The trumpeter rushed out, and I went up and talked with him to cheer him up a bit.

"It's no good!" he said. "I can't stick it any longer! I try to be brave, but I have to give way!"

Then he broke down and fairly cried, and a very pitiful sight it was, for he was only a kiddie, fifteen or sixteen years old.

I was always troubled myself when I saw how these little chaps were upset; but they did not break down through anything like fear—they were not afraid, and were splendid when they were with the men—it was the suffering and the fearful sights they saw that bowled them out.

These trumpeters—mere lads—went through all the marching and fighting that led up to the fearful business at Ypres, and they came out of the business splendidly. Little "Baggie," for example, was right through it from the Aisne, and was up and down with the Siege Artillery all the time. He was present when one of the lieutenants was killed, and when I last heard of him he was still on the move and well; and I sincerely hope that he is all right now, and will come safely home.

I mention these things about the youngsters particularly, because they struck me as being out of the common, and so you notice them more than the ordinary matters.

While speaking of the earlier days of the war, I might say that, after the Marne and the Aisne, when we were going back over ground that we knew and on which we fought, we saw some sickening slaughter scenes, and realised to the full what an awful thing a war like this is.

One very peculiar incident which comes into my mind was the finding of a dead Uhlan in a wood. He had evidently been badly wounded, and had made his way into the wood for safety, but he had died there. When we found him he was sitting in a crouching position. On examining him, we found two postcards which he had written. We could not read them, but, as far as we could tell, they were addressed to women of the same name, but living in different places. We buried the Uhlan in the wood, and handed the postcards to a German officer who had been made prisoner, and he gave us to understand that he would see that they were sent to their destinations when he got a chance to despatch them. That incident was only one of many similar sights we came across in our part of the business.

Transport work, as a rule, was very uncomfortable, because it was mostly done at night, when the roads were very dark, and we had to do as best we could without lights. Anything like an ammunition or supply column was a particular mark for the Germans, and whenever they got the chance they would do their best to find us out; and a favourite way of doing this was to fire a few shots in one place and a few in another, in the hope that we should be drawn and reveal our position. But we didn't give the show away quite so easily as that.

I had many opportunities of seeing the fine work which was done by our armoured trains, and I saw something of the performances of the aeroplanes. I witnessed several air fights, but there was not really a lot to see, because there was so much swift manœuvring. There was plenty of firing at the aircraft, but they are most difficult things to hit. One of the German aeroplanes dropped a bomb on Ypres. It fell on a doctor's house near the town station and exploded, but it did not do any great amount of mischief. It broke the front door and shattered the windows and knocked the place about, but I fancy that it did not hurt or kill anybody.

What was the finest sight I saw while I was at the front? Well, I think the best thing I ever saw was the way some of our lancers scattered a far superior body of Uhlans and made them fly. That was on the retirement from Mons. It was a very bad time, and there were some fearful sights, for the roads leading from the town were crowded with fleeing women and children. In any case it was bad enough to get along the road, but it was infinitely worse to make our way along through the crowds of refugees with our motor-lorries, especially in view of what we carried. To make matters worse, we had got on the wrong road, and it was necessary to turn back. To do this we had to turn round, and, as there were eighty cars, I need not tell you what a business that meant, especially with the enemy harassing us, and I dare say fondly thinking that they had us in a proper grip. The Germans were quite close to us, and firing, and we were ordered to get down and defend the cars. The road at this point was very narrow, and it seemed as if we were trapped, though we were covered by cavalry.

The country thereabouts did not seem very favourable for cavalry work, but it was all right from the point of view of the Uhlans, who, from their horses, potted at us from the brow of the hill on which they stood. The weather was miserable, dull, and it was raining, and, altogether, it was not an exhilarating business. The Uhlans seemed to be having it all their own way; then the scene changed like magic, and that was when the gallant 9th Lancers appeared, to our unspeakable joy. I can claim to understand something in a modest way about cavalry, as an old Imperial Yeoman, and I do know that there was no finer sight ever seen than the spectacle of those splendid fellows of the 9th, who, without any sound of trumpet or any noise, came up and charged the Uhlans. One body of Uhlans was on the brow, two more bodies were in a wood. But these two did not take any active part in the fighting; they seemed to wait till their comrades on the brow had paved the way with us, so that they could swoop down. But the Uhlans did not get a chance to swoop, though they were three to one against our lancers.

Jumping a ditch and galloping across the country, our cavalry were after the Uhlans like the wind. But the Uhlans never stopped to face the lance; they vanished over the brow of the hill, and the fellows who were watching and waiting in the wood vanished, too. They bolted, and must have been thankful to get out of it. All they knew, probably, was that our men came along a road in the wood till they got to a clear part, and that through that opening the 9th were on them like a flash, without firing a shot. They managed to get in amongst the first line of the Germans with the lance and empty some of the saddles, while they themselves had only one or two men bowled over.

I had a splendid view of this brilliant little affair—I should think there were not more than 120 of the 9th—and I shall never forget the way in which the lancers went for the enemy, nor the swiftness with which the boasted Uhlans scuttled off behind the brow. It was an uncommonly fine piece of work, and it saved our column.

The Uhlans had another shot at us two or three days later. They were at quite close range, not more than four or five hundred yards away, but we managed to keep them off and go about our business, which was to reach the Marne and the Aisne, and then start back. We had about a month on the Aisne without making much progress, though our troops were hard at it all the time.

I had got out of Ypres—thankful to go—and had gone towards another town. It was about midday, and we had halted. The hot weather had gone away, and the cold had come. I was walking up and down to keep myself warm. Shells were falling and bursting, as usual, but I did not pay much attention to them. At last one burst about fifty yards away, and a fragment struck me and knocked me round, after which I fell. At first I thought I had been struck by a stone or a brick which somebody had thrown, and it was not for some time that I realised that I had been wounded in the thigh by a piece of shell. I was sent to England in due course, and here I am, in a most comfortable hospital at the seaside, ready to leave for home in two or three days.

My own experience with regard to the wound is not uncommon. It is not easy to say how you have been hit, and I have known men who have been shot through the body and have been quite unable to say whether the bullet went in at the front or the back.

Chapter V – British Gunners as Cave-Dwellers

Corporal E. H. Bean, Royal Field Artillery.

[Sir John French has repeatedly praised the splendid work of the Royal Artillery during the war and glowing tributes to the courage and resourcefulness of British gunners have been paid by the other branches of the Army. Many a critical battle has been turned into a success by the artillery, some of the batteries of which have particularly distinguished themselves. Amongst them is the 134th, of whose officers and men no fewer than five were mentioned in Sir John French's list, published on February 18th, of names of those whom he recommended for gallant and distinguished conduct in the field. This story of some of the work of our gunners is told by Corporal Ernest Henry Bean, of the 134th Field Battery, who was severely wounded and invalided home.]

YOU cannot exaggerate anything in this war. I am of a cheerful and hopeful disposition, but I never thought I should live through the awful business; yet here I am, cheerful still, though shot through both feet, and forced to hop when I want to get from place to place.

I have had some strange adventures during the last few months, and one of the oddest was in this good old Yarmouth. That was when the Germans came and bombed us. But I will tell you about the air raid later. Here are two eighteen-pounder shells, not from the front, but from practice-firing, and it was such shells as these that made havoc amongst the German troops, especially when we got to work on big bodies of them.

The war came upon us so suddenly that even now it seems amazing that I left peaceful England on a summer day and went straight into the very thick of things. There was no waiting, for I sailed from Southampton on the day after Mons was fought, and when we got into action it was at Le Cateau.

We had had a short spell in a rest camp, then we had some hard marching. Throughout the whole of one night we kept at it, and soon after breakfast next morning we were in the thick of one of the most terrible artillery fights that has ever been known. For six mortal hours we were under an incessant shell-fire. The experience itself was enough to leave its mark for ever on your mind, but I shall always remember it because of what happened to our horses. They were not used to this awful business and they stampeded, galloping all over the place, and defying every effort of the drivers to control them. The horses bolted with the waggons and tore madly over the country, taking pretty nearly everything that came in their way. The drivers were on the horses, but they were powerless to control the frightened animals.

The battery itself was in action. I was with the teams—on an open road with half-a-dozen of them, and no protection whatever, for the road ran between open fields. We were a fine target for the Germans, and they saw it and began to shell us hell for leather. The fire was deadly and there is no wonder that the horses bolted.

What was to be done? What could be done except make a dash for shelter? I did my level best to get out of the open and seek shelter. But shelter seemed far away, there was nothing near at hand, but in the distance I saw something that seemed hopeful, so I galloped towards it with my teams. We went furiously along, and as I got nearer to the object I could make out that it was a long brick wall which separated an orchard from the road.

For about a mile, under a constant and furious fire, I dashed on; then I got to the wall, and instantly I drew in as many of the bolting horses as I could lay hands on. It all happened so swiftly that it is not easy to tell how this was done; but I know that I was safely mounted on my own horse when the stampede began, and that I dashed at the bolting animals and grabbed as many as I could, and that I hurried them to the shelter of the wall, and I fancy that they were just about as glad of the protection as I was. The gallop was a mad affair, and very likely it would never have ended as it did if all the shells the Germans fired had burst; but some of them did not explode, though I did not know of this till later, when I picked some of them up from the ground.

While I was in the thick of this exciting business Farrier-Sergeant Scott was rushing about and securing other runaway teams, and he did so well and his work was considered so brilliant and important that the French gave him the decoration of the Legion of Honour.

For the best part of an hour I was under cover of the wall, doing the best I could with the horses, and it was a funny old job to keep them anything like quiet with such a heavy fire going on all the time; yet so complete was the protection that practically no damage was done, the worst that occurred being the shattering of a pair of wheels by a bursting shell.

By the end of the hour both myself and the horses were pretty well settling down; then things calmed down a bit. The Germans appeared to be tired of pounding at us, and perhaps they thought that they had blown us to pieces. At any rate we began to get out of it, and we had no sooner started to do that than the firing instantly re-opened.

There was a village not far away and we made a dash for it; but we were forced to clear out, for the enemy's artillery set the little place on fire and all the stacks and buildings were in flames. There was a good deal of confusion and mixing up of all sorts of troops. I had lost touch with my own lot and was ordered by a captain to join another column for the night, and this I did. I joined the 2nd Brigade Ammunition Column and next day I was with my own battery again, thankful to have got safely through a very dangerous business.

Next day we picked up another position, and had no sooner done that than information came that immense bodies of Germans were on the move in our direction. The outlook was serious, because we were in the open and there was nothing for it except a fight to the death. The Germans were expected along a certain road and we made ready to fire at what is practically point-blank range, using Fuses 0 and 2, so that at 500 and 1000 yards the masses of the enemy would have had the shells bursting amongst them.

We had been through some tough times; but not in any situation which was as unpromising as this. We knew that we could make a long stand, and mow down the Germans as they swept along the open country; but we knew also that in the end vastly superior forces must tell against us; but we held our ground and the stern order went round, "Each take charge of your own gun—and God help us!"

How long that awful strain lasted I cannot tell. It could not have been long, but it seemed an eternity. While it lasted the strain was almost unendurable; then it suddenly snapped, an immense relief came over us and even the bravest and most careless amongst us breathed more freely when we knew that the prospect of almost sure annihilation had passed, for the German hosts, instead of coming by the expected road, had gone another way.

With lighter hearts we limbered up, and day after day, night after night, for eleven days, we kept hard at it, marching and fighting, and whenever we got into action it was against very heavy odds. I was with my own special chum, Sergeant Charlie Harrison, and often enough, especially in the night-time, we would walk alongside our horses and talk as we dragged ourselves along—talk about anything that came into our minds, and all for the sake of keeping awake and not falling down exhausted on the road; yet in spite of everything we could do we would fall asleep. Sometimes we would continue walking while practically asleep—we wanted to save our horses as much as we could—and more than once, when I was riding, I went to sleep and fell out of the saddle. There was one good thing, however, about the shock—it acted as a very fine wakener-up. As for sleeping, when we got the chance of it, we could do that anywhere—in ploughed fields, deep in mud and water, and on the road itself.

All sorts of strange and unexpected things happened. While I was with the Ammunition Column the Engineers were putting all their smartness and skill into the building of a pontoon, and the Germans were specially favouring them with "Coal Boxes." This was my introduction to these big brutes of shells, and it was not pleasant, especially as the column was not more than twenty-five yards from the spot where they were exploding with a terrific roar.

I was standing by my horse, feeling none too comfortable, when a big shell burst and made awful havoc near me. A piece of it came and struck me. I thought I was done for, then I looked around at myself, and found that the two bottom buttons of my greatcoat had been torn away, but that no further damage had been done. I was glad to have got off so easily, and just as pleased to find that the horses had escaped.

At this time we were wanting food pretty badly, so that every ration became precious. We were bivouacked when a file of infantrymen brought in a German prisoner. Of course we gave him a share of pretty well everything there was going, hot tea, bread, biscuits and bully beef, and he did himself well. The prisoner was not exactly the sort to arouse compassion, for he looked well fed and was dressed in a very smart uniform. An officer came up, saw the captive, and said, "Do you think this fellow looks as if he wanted anything?" Truth to tell, the fellow didn't, and as we did want things badly, he was sent somewhere else, and we were not sorry to see him go.

After being kept so constantly on the rack, we had a welcome and remarkable change—we became cave-dwellers. We spent five days and nights in some of the famous caves at Soissons, and had a thoroughly comfortable and happy time. We had a fine chance of resting and enjoying ourselves, and we made the most of it.

Originally these caves were occupied by very primitive people; lately they were used as a French hospital, and the French made all sorts of interesting pictures and carvings on the outsides, by way of decoration, then the British took them over as billets. By nature the caverns were queer gloomy places, but a good deal had been done to make them habitable, such as fitting in doors and windows. There had been a lot of fighting near the caves, with the result that there were graves at the very entrances of some of these uncommon billets; but this had no effect on our spirits. We did not allow ourselves to be depressed. What is the use of that in war-time? The British soldier has the happy knack of making himself at home in all kinds of odd places, and so we did in our billets in the rocks and hillside. We called one of our caves the "Cave Theatre Royal," and another the "Cave Cinema," and many a cheerful performance and fine sing-song we had. The only light we had came from candles, but you can sing just as well by candle-light as you can by big electric lamps, and I don't suppose that ever since the caves were occupied they rang with more cheerful sounds than were heard when the British soldiers were joining in a chorus of the latest popular song from home.

Another great advantage of the caverns was that they gave splendid cover to our guns, and protection to ourselves, so that these five days and nights gave us a real rest and complete change, and we were very sorry when we left them and resumed the work of incessant fighting and marching. We were constantly at the guns, and by way of showing what a fearful business the artillery duels became at times, I may tell you that from a single battery alone—that is, half-a-dozen guns—in one day and night we fired more than 4000 rounds.

It was a vast change from the comfort and safety of the caverns, where never a German shell reached us, to the open again, but we got our quiet times and little recreations still, and one of these intervals we devoted to football. We were at Messines, and so was a howitzer battery, and as we happened to be rather slack, we got up a match. I am keen on football, and things were going splendidly. I had scored two goals and we were leading 3-1, when the game came to a very sudden stop, for some German airmen had seen us running about and had swooped down towards us, with the result that the howitzer chaps were rushed into action and we followed without any loss of time. We took it quite as a matter of course to let the football go, and pound away at the

Germans, who had so suddenly appeared. It was getting rather late, so we gave the enemy about fifty rounds by way of saying good-night. We always made a point of being civil in this direction; but our usual dose for good-night was about fifteen rounds.

Talking of football recalls sad memories. On Boxing Day, 1913, when I and an old chum were home on leave, I played in a football match, and at the end of the game a photograph was taken of the team. On last Boxing Day, if the roll of the team had been called, there would have been no answer in several cases—for death and wounds have claimed some of the eleven. Little did we think when we were being grouped for the picture that it was the last muster for us as a team.

We had got through the tail end of summer and were well into autumn, and soon the gloom of November was upon us, then came my change of luck and I was knocked out. It was November 2, and almost as soon as it was daylight we were in the thick of an uncommonly furious artillery duel, one of the very worst I have seen. The Germans seemed to be making a special effort that morning. They had got our position pretty accurately, and they fired so quickly and had the range so well that we were in a real hell of bursting shrapnel, indeed, the fragments were so numerous that it is little short of a miracle that we were not wiped out.

We had not been long in action when a shell burst on the limber-pole, smashed it in halves, penetrated through the wheel, blew the spokes of the wheel away and shot me some distance into the air. For a little while I had no clear idea of what had happened, then I found that three of us had been wounded. My right boot had been blown to shreds, and there was a hole right through the left boot. So much I saw at once—a mess of blood and earth and leather; but of the extent of my wounds I knew very little, nor did I trouble much about them at the time. The first thing I did was to get into the main pit by the side of the gun, the captain and one or two chums helping me, and there, though the pain of my wounds was terrible, I laughed and chatted as best I could, and I saw how the battery kept at it against big odds.

Number 1, Sergeant Barker, who was in charge of the gun, had been struck by a piece of shrapnel, which had fractured his leg; but though that was quite enough to knock him out of time, he never flinched or faltered. He held on to his gun, and went on fighting pretty much as if nothing had happened. Number 2, Gunner Weedon, had been wounded through the thigh, a bad injury about three inches long being caused; but he, too, held gamely on.

I tried to crawl out of the pit; but could not do so, and I passed the time by trying to cheer my chums, just as they did their best to help me to keep my own spirits up.

The sergeant found time occasionally to turn round and ask how I was getting on.

"It's all right, old Bean," he shouted cheerily. "Keep quiet. We can manage without you." And he went on firing, while the officers continued to give orders and encourage the men.

I was getting very thirsty and craved for a drink; but I saw no prospect of getting either water or anything else at such a time.

The sergeant noticed my distress and gave me the sweetest drink I ever tasted, and that was a draught from his own canteen. He managed to stop firing for a few seconds while he did this—just long enough to sling his canteen round, let me take a pull, and sling it back. I learned afterwards that throughout the whole of that day, in that inferno of firing and bursting shells, the sergeant stuck to his gun and kept it at. For his courage and tenacity he has been awarded the Distinguished Conduct Medal, and no man has ever more fully deserved it.

I was lying in the gun pit for about an hour, then a doctor came and my wounds were dressed, but there was no chance of getting away for the time being, so I had to wait till the firing ceased. At last a stretcher was brought, and I was carried into a barn which was at the rear of our battery. One of the bearers was Sergeant E. Leet, the right-back in our battery team. He left the fight to bear a hand with me, and as soon as I was safely in the barn he returned to his post. He had no sooner done that than he too was struck down by a wound in the ankle and had to be invalided home.

"We were in a real hell of burning shrapnel."

When I was carried away the major and the sergeant-major said good-bye, and I rather think they expected that that was the last they would ever see of me. I certainly felt bad, and I daresay I looked it; but I was quite cheerful. I particularly felt it when I passed my chum, Charlie Harrison, because for more than six years we had kept together without a break. We shouted good-bye as we passed, and I did not know whether I should ever see him again.

When I reached the barn I wanted to get back to the battery, to be at my own gun again, to bear a hand once more in the fighting that was still going on and seemed as if it would never stop; but when I tried to stand up I collapsed, through pain and loss of blood. Soon after this I heard that

Charlie Harrison too had been wounded. He was struck on the neck just after I was carried away from the gun pit and had shouted good-bye to him; but he bandaged himself and refused to leave the battery.

What became of him? Why, he got home from the front a day or two ago, and you've just seen him. There he is. And let me show you this shattered foot, to let you see how it is that I'm forced to hop when I want to get about.

And now to get back to the air raid on the East Coast, which to me and other soldiers from the front who saw it, was an extraordinary experience, though I fancy that we took it more or less as a matter of course, because you so soon get used to that kind of thing.

I had scarcely settled down at home when one night there was a fearful commotion, caused by dull explosions. I was a bit taken aback, for I knew what the sounds meant, and thought that I had done with the Germans and fighting for a spell at any rate.

As soon as the sound of the explosions was heard, people rushed into the streets—the most dangerous thing they could do—to see what it all meant, and there were cries that the Germans had come.

So they had. They had come in a gas-bag or two, and were dropping bombs on the good old town, which was lighted as usual, though that was soon altered.

I hopped into the street—hopping is the only thing I can do at present—and there I found that there was intense excitement and that women in particular were badly scared. But really the thing did not upset me at all—it was mere child's play compared with what I had been through, so I made myself useful, and hopped away and bought some brandy, which suited some of the scared people very well—so well that there wasn't a drop left for myself.

The raid was soon over, and so was the scare, and I hopped back to the house. There have been several frantic alarms since then, and more than once I have been shaken out of my sleep and told that the Germans have come again;

but all I have said has been that it will take something far worse than a German gas-bag raid to make me turn out of bed in the middle of the night.

A French Nieuport biplane fighter plane

Chapter VI – With the "Fighting Fifth"

Private W. G. Long, 1st Battalion East Surrey

[One of the battalions which composed the 5th Division of the British Expeditionary Force was the 1st East Surrey Regiment. It was on the 5th Division that so much of the heavy fighting fell on the way to the Aisne, and in that heavy fighting the East Surreys suffered very severely. This story is told by Private W. G. Long, who rejoined his regiment from the Reserve. He has been wounded by shrapnel, and has permanently lost the use of his right arm.\]

WHEN I went out with my old battalion, the Young Buffs, we were more than 1,300 strong. When I came back, after six weeks' fighting, we had lost more than half that number. This simple fact will show you what the East Surreys have done during the war, as part of the famous "Fighting Fifth" which has been so greatly praised by Sir John French.

I had got up to start my day's work after the August Bank Holiday; but that day's work was never done, for the postman brought the mobilisation papers, and off I went to Kingston, after kissing my wife and baby good-bye. Many a fine fellow who marched off with me is sleeping in or near a little forest which we called "Shrapnel Wood." That was near Missy, where we crossed the Aisne on rafts.

We lost our first man soon after we landed in France, and before we met the Germans. That was at Landrecies, where we went into French barracks, and were told off into rooms which we called rabbit-hutches, because they were so small—no bigger than a little kitchen at home. We were crowded into these, and the only bed we had was a bit of straw on the floor. The nights were bitterly cold, but the days were hot enough to melt us; so we had a bathing parade, and had a fine old time in the canal till one of our men was missed.

I looked around, and saw that one of our fellows was having artificial respiration tried on him. He came round, and then he told us that another man had gone under the water. Then began a really first-class diving display, many of our chaps plunging into the canal to try to find the missing soldier.

At last one of the divers rose and shouted, "I've got him!" And, sure enough, he had brought a poor chap to the surface. Lots of strong arms were stretched out, and in a few seconds the rescued man was got on to the bank, and every effort was made to bring him back to life. But nothing could be done. The man was drowned, and we buried him. This little tragedy threw quite a gloom over us till we moved away.

I am going to tell of a few of the things that happened and affected me personally. They took place mostly when we were retiring, and some of them occurred in the early days, when we were forging along in fearfully bad weather. We were soaked to the skin, and at night did our best to get some sort of shelter by building up the stacks of corn that had been cut for drying, but it was no use. The rain came through so heavily that we gave the task up, and waited for daylight again. When the day came it brought another rain of shells and bullets with it. The place got too warm for us, so we had to leave and retire again. We went on, getting as much shelter as we could; and then we had to halt, and here the sorry discovery was made that we had not a round of ammunition left. At this time there were advancing towards us some men in khaki, and our sergeant, thinking they were our own men, told us not to fire at them.

The order was not necessary, seeing that we had nothing to fire with. As soon as these men got level with us on our flank they opened fire, and then we knew that they were Germans, who had stripped some of our men, or had picked up British caps and greatcoats which had been thrown aside.

In this desperate position a man who belonged to the Cornwall Light Infantry was shot just below the left ear. He was knocked down, but got up, and kept saying, "Help me! Help me!"

I shouted to him to lie down and keep under cover, but he took no notice, and kept on calling for help. He came up to me, and when he was near enough I pulled him down and forced him to lie on the ground. All this time there was a very heavy fire. We were getting shots from the front and on our flanks, and there was nothing for it but to get away as best we could.

I could not bear the thought of leaving this Cornwall man where he was, so I took him up and began to carry him, but it was very slow going. It was all uphill, the ground was sodden with rain, and I had to force a way through a field of turnips, which were growing as high as my knees. It was bad enough to make one's own way through such a tangle as that; but I am young and strong, and I managed to make progress, although I was hit five different times—not hurt, but struck, a shot, for instance, hitting my cap, another my water-bottle, and another the sleeve of my coat.

After going a long distance, as it seemed, and feeling utterly exhausted, I put my man down under what I thought was safe shelter. I wanted to give him a drink, but I could not do so, as the shot-hole in my water-bottle had let the water run to waste.

At last we reached a roadway, where we saw some more of our men, who had got there before us, and had commandeered a horseless cart and filled it with wounded men.

I got the wounded man into the cart, and then off we all went. It was as much as we could manage to get the cart along, for it was such a great big thing; but we worked it willingly, the officers taking their turn in the shafts.

We dragged the cart along the heavy roads, but it was such hard going that we saw that we should be forced to get a horse from somewhere; so we looked around at the first farm we came to—and a sorry place it was, with everything in confusion, and the animals about suffering terribly and starving—and there we found a horse of the largest size.

With great difficulty we got together bits of harness, string and rope, and tied the horse in the shafts with the ropes for traces, and when we had finished we did not know whether we had harnessed the horse or tied the cart on to it. Anyway, we got along very well after that.

The cart had amongst its wounded an infantry officer who had been saved by one of our fellows, though the officer belonged to another regiment. He had got entangled in some barbed wire, and, as he had been wounded in the leg, he could not move either one way or the other. He was absolutely helpless, and under a heavy fire.

Our fellow went out and got to the helpless officer, and, by sticking at it and doing all he could, being himself pretty badly cut in the operation, he freed the officer from the entanglement, and carried him safely up to the cart. We were getting on very nicely with our little contrivance when we ran into the 2nd Dragoons, but we soon left them behind us, and found ourselves amongst some of our own transport. We joined up with it, adding another and a very strange waggon to the column, and on we went until we reached a large town and halted.

During the whole of this time I had been carrying a canteen which had belonged to a Frenchman. It was quite a big canteen, and I kept it filled with apples, of which we got an enormous number, and on which at times we had practically to live for two or three days together.

We had reached a stage of fighting when we had to make continuous short rushes against the Germans, under hails of shrapnel. In making these rushes it often happened that we sheltered behind a little sort of earthwork which we threw up. We just made a bit of head cover and lay behind that; but sometimes this head cover could not be made, and that was where I scored with my Frenchman's canteen.

During one of our rushes shrapnel burst right over my head, and one fellow said to me, "I wouldn't carry that thing, George, if I were you." But, having kept it for so long, I was not going to throw it away.

Away we went. I was carrying the canteen in my left hand, and my rifle in the right; but I changed them over, and I had no sooner done that than crash came a shell, and, in bursting, a fragment hit the canteen, and took a great piece out of it. I should have been badly wounded myself, but I had filled the canteen with earth, and so it had protected me and acted as a first-rate cover. The man who was on my right received a nasty wound.

After this we had to advance over open country, where there was not so much as a blade of grass for cover. We went on till we reached a ditch, which was full of water. Some of us had to wade through it, but others, by going farther back, were able to cross a tiny footbridge—one of those narrow planks which only allow one man at a time to cross. The Germans had a machine-gun trained at this little bridge so we lost no time in getting off it. It was here that our captain was mortally wounded by a shot, and we had other casualties in crossing the bridge.

From this point we had to climb to the top of a hill, which was so steep that we had to dig our fixed bayonets into the ground to help us up. There was a wood at the top of the hill, and there we took shelter; but we had no sooner got amongst the trees than the shrapnel was on us again, causing many casualties.

There were many funny incidents at this place, and one I particularly remember was that there were three of us in a sort of heap, when a piece of shell dropped just alongside. There was not any great force in it, because before falling the piece had struck a tree; but, as it dropped, fellows started turning up the collars of their coats, and rolling themselves into balls—just as if things of that sort could make any difference to a bursting shell; but it is amusing to see what men will do at such a time as that.

From this wood we got into what seemed a wide roadway between two other woods, and here we were under a never-ending rain of bullets, which hit the trees, sending splinters all over us, cutting branches off and ploughing up the ground on every side. One of our officers said, "Keep your heads down, lads," and he had scarcely got the words out of his mouth when he was shot in the body and killed, and we had to leave him where he fell.

So heavy and continuous was the fire that we could not get on between these two woods, and we had to try another way; so we started to go through a vineyard, but we were forced to lie down. We sheltered as best we could amongst the vines, with bullets coming and actually cutting off bunches of grapes. Like good British soldiers, we made the best of the business, for we were both hungry and thirsty, and we devoured a good many of the bunches that were knocked off by the German bullets.

After this we got into an orchard, but we did not remain there long, as the place was later on blown to smithereens. We hung on to the orchard till it was dark, then we advanced farther into the wood, and again got through into the open, and lay down to try and get some sleep; but that was almost impossible, because it was raining and perishingly cold, and we had nothing at all for cover. Then, in whispers, we were ordered to get out as silently as we possibly could.

At first I could not understand the meaning of this secrecy, but it soon became known that we had been actually sleeping amongst the enemy, though we were not aware of this until we were again on the move. We crept about like a lot of mice, till we reached a village, where we were to get some breakfast.

We were settling down, and making ourselves comfortable under a wall which gave us some cover. There were some men from another regiment with us, and we thought we were going to have a good time, for we had got hold of some biscuits and jam. Then over the wall came a shell, which exploded and wounded about seven men from the other regiment. We did not stop for any more breakfast, and some of the men who had had nothing to eat did not trouble to get anything, and they went without food for the rest of the day.

We went back to the wood, and there we soon again found the Germans, and plenty of them. We fired at them for all we were worth, after which we advanced a little, and came across so many dead that we had to jump over them every pace we took. One thing which particularly struck me then, and which I remember now, was the great size of some of these German soldiers. At a little distance they looked just like fallen logs.

After that our officer called us together to wait for reinforcements. I thought I would have a look around me, and while I was doing so I saw one German running off to our left, about fifteen yards away. I took aim and fired, and down he went. I got down on my knee and unloaded my rifle, when I saw another German going in the same direction. I was just getting ready to take aim again, but this time I did not fire—in fact, I did not even get to the aim, for I felt something hit my arm.

For the moment I thought that some chap behind me had knocked me with his rifle or his foot. I turned round, but there was no one behind me, so I concluded that I had been hit. I stood up, and then my arm began to wobble, and the blood streamed out of my sleeve. Someone shouted, "You've got it, George." And I replied: "Yes; in the arm somewhere, but where I don't know."

I did my best to get back again, and then a fellow came, and ripped the sleeve open and dressed my arm, and there was all my elbow joint laid open, and some of the bones broken. This chap wanted to take me back to the village, but I said I was all right, although in a sense I was helpless. We started going back, and we got to the first house, where we saw a poor old man and his daughter who had been there all through the fighting. The place was filled with wounded, and the two were doing their best for them.

I asked for a drink, for I was almost dying of thirst, and I got some whisky. While I was drinking it a shell burst in the middle of the road, and sent the mud and stones everywhere; so I shifted my quarters, and went along to a big house which had been a fine place, but it had been pulled to pieces, and was now being used as a hospital. The place itself gave no protection, but we found a cellar and crowded into it, and there we watched the Germans blowing the temporary hospital to pieces.

The night came, and it was terrible to hear the poor chaps moaning with pain. I was in pain myself now, but my sufferings were a mere nothing compared with those of some of the men around me. It seemed as if the day would never break, but at last it came, and by that time some of the poor fellows who had been making such pitiful noises were no more. Sometime after that, however, I got away in a field ambulance.

When we were at Le Cateau many spies were caught. I saw several of them. They were young chaps, dressed up as women and as boys and girls, and it was not very easy to detect them. One was disguised as a woman, with rather a good figure. I saw this interesting female when she was captured by our artillery. The gunners had their suspicions aroused, with the result that they began to knock the lady about a bit, and her wig fell off. Then her figure proved to be not what it seemed, for the upper front part of it was composed of two carrier-pigeons! I did not see the end of that batch of spies, but a battery sergeant-major afterwards told me that they had been duly shot.

One of the most extraordinary things I saw was the conduct of a man who had had his right arm shot off from above the elbow. I was standing quite near him, and expected that he would fall and be helpless. Instead of doing that, he turned his head and looked at the place where the arm should have been. I suppose he must have been knocked off his balance by what had happened. At any rate, he gave a loud cry, and instantly started to run as fast as I ever saw a man go. Two or three members of the Royal Army Medical Corps at once gave chase, with the object of securing him and attending to him. The whole lot of them disappeared over some rising ground, and what happened to them I do not know.

"I took him up and began to carry him."

I saw many fellows who had queer tales to tell of what had happened to them. One chap, a rifleman, who was in the ship coming home, was so nervous that the slightest noise made him almost jump out of his skin. And well it might, for his nerves had been shattered. A shell had buried itself in the ground just in front of him and exploded, blowing him fifteen feet into the air, and landing him in a bed of mud. He was so completely stunned that he lay there for about eight hours, scarcely moving, though he was not even scratched. He came round all right, but was a nervous wreck, and had to be invalided.

Chapter VII - The Victory of the Marne

Corporal G. Gilliam, Coldstream Guards.

[One of the most moving statements in the earlier official reports dealing with the war was that about the fighting at Mons and elsewhere, which cost us 6000 men, and no paragraph was more stirring than that relating to Landrecies, a quiet little French town on the Sambre. "In Landrecies alone," the report said, "a German infantry brigade advanced in the closest order into the narrow street, which they completely filled. Our machine-guns were brought to bear on this target from the end of the town. The head of the column was swept away, a frightful panic ensued, and it is estimated that no fewer than 800 to 900 dead and wounded Germans were lying in this street alone." The story of that furious combat and the subsequent operations on the Marne is told by Corporal G. Gilliam, of the Coldstream Guards. On September 6, in conjunction with the French, the British assumed the offensive, and, after a four days' desperate struggle, which is known as the Battle of the Marne, the Germans were driven back to Soissons, with enormous losses.]

IT was early on the afternoon of August 26 when we entered Landrecies, which is a little garrison town, consisting mostly of a single street in which there are three cross-roads. We were billeted in the people's houses, and for the first time in three days we had a drop of tea and a bit of dinner in comfort, and to crown our satisfaction we were told we could lie down and rest, but we were to have our bayonets fixed and rifles by our sides and kits ready to put on.

We were soon down to it and sound asleep. It was about eight o'clock when some of us woke, and after a smoke were off to sleep again, but not for long, for almost immediately we heard the sound of a motor-cycle, and knew that the rider was travelling at a terrific rate.

Nearer and nearer came the sound, and the rider himself swept round the corner of the street. He never stopped nor slackened speed; he simply shouted one word as he vanished, and that was "Germans!" Only one word, but enough.

Rifles in hand, we rushed to the top of the street and lined the three cross-roads, lying down. Our officer, who was standing up behind us, said, "Lie still, men"; and we did—perfectly still, not a man moving. All at once, out of the darkness, an officer came and cried in English to our commander, "Surrender!"

"We don't surrender here!" our officer answered. "Take that!"—and instantly shot him through the head with his revolver.

Our officer's shot had scarcely died away when crash went a German artillery gun, and a lyddite shell burst right over us. This was our first experience of lyddite, and the fumes nearly choked us.

"Lie still, boys—don't move!" said our officer; and we lay low.

Just then, from the opposite direction, we heard the sound of horses and a waggon, in the distance, it seemed; but soon it was very near, and to our great joy there dashed up the street one of the guns of the 17th Field Battery. There was a shout of "Into action! Left wheel!" And in truly magnificent style that gun was almost instantly laid and ready for action.

Shells now came upon us rapidly, wounding several of our men; but our maxim gunners had got to work, and very soon enormous numbers of Germans were put beyond the power of doing any further mischief.

Many splendid things were done that night at Landrecies; but there was nothing finer than the work of our maxim-gunner Robson, who was on our left. Our machine-guns were by now at our end of the town, and they had a solid mass of Germans to go at. Robson was sitting on his stool, and as soon as the officer ordered "Fire!" his maxim hailed death. It literally was a hail of fire that met the packed Germans, and swept down the head of the column, so that the street was choked in an instant with the German dead. Those who lived behind pushed on in desperation—shoved on by the masses still further behind, the darkness being made light by the fire of the maxims and the enemy's rifles. Those behind, I say, pressed on, with fearful cries, but only to be mown down and shattered, so that the street became more than ever glutted with the dead and wounded. The Germans were thrown into frenzy, and if sheer weight of men could have driven the head of the column on to us not a British soldier could have lived that night at Landrecies.

Meanwhile, we had been ordered to hold our fire. There were only 600 of us opposed to an immense body of Germans; but the maxims were doing annihilating work, and the artillery had got into action.

When the gun of the 17th had got the order to fire we heard a gunner shout: "Watch me put that gun out of action!"—meaning a German gun which had been brought up and laid against us. He fired, and the most marvellous thing happened, for the shell from it went right down the muzzle of the German weapon and shattered it to pieces.

Then we heard a shout, and before we could look round about 4000 German infantry were charging us, with horns blowing and drums beating—adding to the fearful din.

"Don't shoot, boys," shouted our officer, "till I give the word!"

On the living mass of Germans came. They rushed up to within 80 yards of us; then the order rang out: "Fire!"

Again the Germans got it—fifteen rounds to the minute from each rifle, for the front rank men had their loading done for them. As soon as a rifle was emptied it was handed to the rear and a fresh loaded rifle was handed back. In this way the rifles were kept from getting too hot, and an incessant fire was poured into the Germans.

In spite of this hail, a few Germans managed to break through their walls of dead and wounded. One of them, disguised as a French officer, and wanting us to think he had been a prisoner, but had just broken away from the Germans, rushed up to Robson and patted him on the shoulder and said: "Brave fellow!" And with that he whipped round his sword and killed our maxim gunner on the spot; but he himself was instantly shot down by our enraged fellows.

There was another case of treachery, this time, unhappily, from inside our ranks. Our guide, a man claiming to be a Frenchman, at about one o'clock in the morning, turned traitor, and went and told the Germans how many there were of us, and by way of indicating our position he fired a haystack; but he had no sooner done that than two bullets settled him.

One of our corporals dashed away to put the fire out, but before he reached the haystack he was killed. It was at this time that Private Wyatt, of my company, rushed out—everything was done at a rush—and brought in a wounded officer. The colonel, who was on his horse, and saw what had happened, said: "Who is that brave man?" He was told, and afterwards Wyatt was taken before the general and recommended for a decoration.

Hour after hour, all through the time of darkness, and until daylight came, that terrible fight went on. For seven long hours a few hundred British Guards had kept at bay an enormous body of Germans—and at the end of the firing we had killed far more than the whole of our force numbered when the battle began. We had given them wholesale death from our machine-guns, our rifles, and our artillery, and they had faced it—they had been driven on to it. Now they were to have the bayonet.

We gave them two charges; but they didn't stop long, for as soon as they saw the cold steel on the ends of our rifles they were off like a shot, throwing down a lot of rifles and equipment. When this happened it was between five and six o'clock on the morning of the 27th, and we then got the order to retire.

We were told that we had lost 126 in killed and wounded. That was a heavy list, but not so big as we had expected, bearing in mind the furious nature of the fight. The marvel was that we had not been wiped out, and we should certainly have been in a very serious state if it had not been for the 17th Field Battery. There is this to be said, too: if the Germans had broken through our lines it would have meant that, in all probability, the whole Second Division of our army would have been cut up.

We fell in and were soon on the march again, retiring, and we marched as fast as we could go till we halted at a rather large town about ten miles from Landrecies. Here we were in clover, in a way of speaking, because we sheltered in a clay-pit where the French had been making bricks, and we all sat down and waited for our tea of German shells.

They soon came and we were on the move again, and we were constantly at it, retiring and fighting, until we halted about thirty miles from Paris; then we were told that after retiring another dozen miles it would be our turn to advance.

Didn't we cheer? It was glorious to hear we were going to chase the Germans instead of their chasing us. At this time we had our first wash for a fortnight, and it was as good as having a thousand pounds given to us.

The fiercest fighting of the war has taken place on Sundays, and it was on a Sunday that the Battle of the Marne began. The Germans had had the biggest surprise of their lives on a Sunday, and that was at Mons. Though we had been kept on the go because they outnumbered us so hopelessly, we mauled them mercilessly on the retreat, teaching them many bitter lessons. When we got to the Marne and were able to tackle them on equal terms, they scarcely had a look in. The Germans had almost reached the forts of Paris, and, I daresay, had their bands ready to play them into the city. Soon, however, they were hurrying back on their tracks a good deal faster than they had come. We heard the German bands playing a good many times, but every time we heard the music it was farther away from Paris.

We covered such big tracks of country, and saw so many great happenings, that it is the most difficult thing in the world to know where to start a story of the Marne; but I will come down to the time just before the battle, when we were still retiring, and had got used to marching twenty or twenty-five miles a day. We had left the Germans very sore for coming too close to us, and we had gone through a small town and entered a great wood.

While we were in the wood I had to fall out. Almost instantly I heard the sound of talking which wasn't English, and in the distance I saw six Germans coming after me as hard as they could. I thought it was all up with me, but I said "Come on, chum, let's clear!"—"chum" being my rifle, which I had placed on the ground. I snatched it up and sprang behind a tree, and felt fairly safe. It's wonderful what a feeling of security a good rifle and plenty of ammunition give you. I waited till the Germans got within a hundred yards of me; then with a good aim I fetched down two; but my position was becoming very critical, as the other four dodged from tree to tree, watching for a chance to pot me, and it looked very much as if they wouldn't have long to wait. I don't know what would have happened, but to my intense relief three men of the 17th Field Battery, which was passing, rushed up and shouted, "Don't move. We'll have 'em!"

By this time the four Germans were within about fifty yards, continually sniping at me—how I blessed them for being such bad shots!—and at last they came out into the open and made straight in my direction. But they only dashed about twenty yards, for my rescuers put "paid" to the four of them, and saved me from being made a prisoner and worse, far worse, for by that time we had seen proof enough of the monstrous things they did to men they captured— things you might expect from savages, but certainly not from soldiers of a nation that boasts so much of its civilisation.

The last day of our retirement was September 4, and on that day we never saw the enemy. We had crossed and recrossed the River Marne, and had blown up bridges as we retired; but the Germans threw their own bridges over the river with amazing speed, and kept up the pursuit. Sometimes they overdid their zeal, and were a trifle too quick for their own comfort.

We had blown up two bridges that crossed the Marne, one a railway bridge and the other a fine stone structure. I was one of the last of our men to cross the stone bridge before the engineers, who had made it ready for destruction. The bridge ran between two high banks, so that it was a considerable height above the water. When the explosion took place there was a tremendous shattering roar, almost like a salvo of Black Marias, then a crashing and grinding and thudding as the middle of the bridge was utterly wrecked, and fell into the river, leaving an immense gap between the banks. The work of months, costing thousands upon thousands of pounds, had been smashed in a few seconds.

I was looking back at the ruins when I saw a motor-car, with several Germans in it, tearing after us, meaning to cross the bridge as we had done. The car came on at a tremendous speed, and the Germans in it must have had eyes only for us and none for the road in front of them, for they rushed on right into the blank space, and before they knew what was happening, the car was in the river.

We had had battle after battle, each one in itself enough to make a long story. We had fought and marched in the fearful August heat, and had been thankful when we could lie down with a little heap of sand or a sheaf of corn as a pillow. At last we were so near Paris that the forts opened fire, and that was the beginning of what I'm sure will be the end of the Germans.

Now at last we were in touch with the French, and we got the Germans in a proper grip. The French got round the Germans and turned them towards Coulommiers, a town on the Marne; then the British took the job on and drove the Germans through the town. That part of the work fell largely on the Guards, and what we were doing was being done, of course, over an enormous stretch of country by other British and French troops.

We had got to the night of September 5 and were lying in trenches which we had dug along a canal bank about Coulommiers. We waited for the Germans to come, and they came in fine style. It was getting dark and we could make out three of their aeroplanes sweeping in the air like big birds. We had seen a good deal of the German aeroplanes by this time and knew what to expect. These were trying to find out our positions, so that they could signal to their gunners and give them the range.

"Before they knew what was happening the car was in the river."

Suddenly the aeroplanes dropped some balls of blue fire, and very pretty the fireworks looked; but we hadn't time to admire them, because the German artillery instantly opened fire on us with such fury that we felt the very ground shake as we lay in our trenches.

Under cover of their guns the Germans—the 32nd Infantry Brigade, I think it was—dashed up to the other side of the canal bank and blazed away at us; but we blazed harder at them. We gave them a fair hell of rifle fire and very soon they were forced to clear out, leaving the whole of the canal bank littered with their dead and wounded.

A fine little "tiffey" we had at the Marne was a rearguard action, in which there was one of those British cavalry and infantry charges that have shaken a lot of the Germans to pieces, especially the Uhlans, who are a pretty poor crowd in spite of all their boasting.

Our scouts had returned with the news that the Germans were entrenched about a mile and a half away, on the bank of the Marne. We got the order to extend the usual three paces, and our advance guard went out, while our main body lay down. Our advance guard had gone about 900 yards when the German infantry opened fire. We took it up, and there was a ceaseless rattle. We kept the Germans well employed, and our advance guard were pouring in a proper good peppering. But there was a little surprise in store for them. We had with us a couple of the magnificent British cavalry regiments—the Scots Greys and the 16th Lancers, and they swept on till they got to a little wood, where they had the Germans on the left wing of their rearguard, fairly at their mercy. When they were ready for the charge the signal was given to our advance guard, and, with a perfect roar of cheering, the British cavalry and infantry hurled themselves on the Germans, a tremendous weight of horse and man. The Greys and the 16th fairly thundered over the earth, and the Guards rushed up in splendid style, though we had our heavy packs, and in such hot weather a big weight adds enormously to the terrific work of charging. But you don't think of heat or weight at such a time—you feel only the thrill and excitement of the battle and have the joy of knowing that you are settling the account of a suffering and outraged nation.

Cavalry and Guards got in amongst the Germans and fairly scattered them. I got one German in the back and another sideways, and all around me chums were doing the same, while the cavalry were cutting the Germans down everywhere. Limbs literally flew about as they were lopped off with the sword, and Germans in the open and in the trenches—for we routed them out—fell to the bayonet.

That was a fierce and bloody "tiffey," and there have been many like it. At the end of it we had settled that particular German rearguard and had a nice bag of prisoners. A lot of these prisoners were glad to be out of the business; most of the Germans we captured seemed to feel like that, and I remember hearing one of them—an officer—say, in good English, "Thank God I'm caught! Now I shall not starve anymore!"

Talking of charges, I might tell you that there is a great difference between the British and the German ways of doing it. The Germans make as much noise as possible—a perfect devil of a row, with drums thumping and trumpets sounding, and, of course, their banners flying. We carry no colours into action (we leave them at home), we have no drum-thumping and no bugles sounding—often enough the signal for a charge is just something like a hand wave or a word of command; but that answers all practical purposes and starts us on the business as quickly and full of fire as any amount of noise.

When we had got through our first rearguard action we thought we had driven the Germans to the other side of the Marne and got them fairly on the move back to Berlin; but to our surprise we were attacked by a strong force of their cavalry, who had been in ambush not a thousand yards away. The German horsemen came on us at a full gallop and swept on until they were about two hundred yards away. At this particular spot there were Guards, Worcesters, and Camerons, and it looked very much as if the Germans would dash up and do a lot of mischief.

The commander of the Worcesters shouted, "Fix bayonets! Make sure of your men."

On came the German cavalry, with a roar and a rattle, until they were less than a hundred yards away; then we let go and the troopers tumbled out of their saddles like ninepins. The going was too hard for German cavalry, and as one of their officers shouted an order, they wheeled round and made off, rushing, as they supposed, for a safe place and a way out; but they galloped straight up to a spot where some French artillery were in position.

The Germans thundered on towards their fancied safety; then there were crashes from the French artillery, and shells went plump into the horsemen and practically annihilated them. Horses and men were shattered, and of those who escaped the French took about one hundred and fifty prisoners. It was a fine little performance, and helped us to fix in our memories the first meeting with the Frenchmen on the Marne.

The artillery fire on the Marne was awful in its destructiveness and earsplitting in its noise—sometimes the very air seemed to be solid matter that was broken into chunks and knocked about you; but we soon got used to it all, and laughed and smoked and joked in the trenches, where, at the back, we had dug-outs which we called rabbit-hutches. These were shelter-places, well covered at the top, and were most useful protections against shells. When the enemy's fire became too hot we would go into our rabbit-hutches.

About noon on the 6th we had re-formed and advanced to the bank of the river, and there we found that we were opposed to a large body of Germans and that they had howitzer batteries with them. These howitzers do deadly mischief, and the fumes from their lyddite shells are perfectly poisonous—they spread through a good big patch of air and suffocate the men. It was about four o'clock in the afternoon when the Germans began to pour into us a fearful fire, and we were enfiladed; but our trenches gave us some fine shelter, and the Germans did not have their own way for long, nor did they do much damage at that point. Here again the British had ready one more of the many surprises that the Germans met with on the banks of the Marne. One of our batteries of short howitzers, four guns, went along the river bank and hid in some bushes on the right of the German howitzers, while a battery of our field artillery dashed up and took a commanding position which got the Germans between two fires. Then the command was given, "Ten rounds rapid fire!"

But ten rounds were not needed—only four were fired before the German battery was put to rest. But the crippling of the German howitzers did not seem to have much effect on the enemy at that point, for they rushed up more of the infantry, which, brought along by immense numbers of trains and motors, literally swarmed over the countryside.

At this time we renewed our acquaintance with some of the Germans who were known to us as the "drop-shots." I believe there is only one brigade of them in the German Army, and I will do them the justice to say that they are very good at the game. They kneel down, and putting the butt of the rifle on the thigh, fire in the air at an angle of about forty-five degrees. The bullet makes a big arc and drops right on top of you in such places as trenches. These "drop-shots" were about four hundred yards away, but they hadn't got just the right range of us and the bullets plugged into the wrong places.

The "drop-shots" tried their queer game on us for about half an hour, but finding that they could not damage us, they stopped, especially as we were beginning to shift them out of their positions. There was some furious rifle firing between the troops entrenched on both banks of the Marne, and often enough the reddened water bore away many a dead soldier.

The fighting was always most fierce when the Germans were in masses and hurled their regiments against us in their attempt to hack their way through to Paris. Any street fighting that came about was sure to be terrific, and one of the most furious of the fights took place in the streets of Coulommiers, a town similar to Reading.

Coulommiers, of course, was almost entirely given up to troops, for the inhabitants had been warned by us to leave and get as far away from the Germans as they could go. Poor souls, they did not need much persuading, knowing what they did of German "culture," and, carrying with them only such few oddments as they could quickly collect, they fled, the roads leading to Paris being thick with them. During this fighting in Coulommiers there was such brilliant moonlight that you could see almost well enough to shoot a rabbit.

It was about eight o'clock at night when we got to Coulommiers. We were just going to stop to have some food when the Germans put two big shells into us, killing four of our men, and wounding fourteen. We jumped up, fixed bayonets, and rushed for the Germans; but we were brought up by some more shells, and for a couple of hours the guns were banging at us. Fortunately the shells had a bit too long a range, and instead of hitting us they went over the back of us.

We lay down until ten o'clock, when the order was given to prepare to charge. Up again we sprang—we were getting used to charging—and made another rush, running as hard as we could down the street for a hundred yards, then lying flat in the roadway.

All this time the Germans were pouring in on us a fire which, if it had been accurate, would have swept us out of existence. But it was very poor stuff, and we were lucky enough to escape with the loss of a very few men. We were lying down for five minutes, then we were up and off again, dashing along the main street.

It was a rousing bit of work, and we gloried in it, especially when, from every doorway in the street, Germans dashed out and made a bolt for their lives. They had been firing at us from bedroom windows, and tore frantically downstairs and out of doorways when they saw that we were fairly on the job and after them.

That bolting gave us just the chance we wanted. We drove after the flying Germans as hard as we could go, and being big and powerful men, with plenty of weight in us, we literally picked some of them up on the bayonets. We rushed them through the town and out of it; then we came across a gang of Germans who were no good at all. They had looted all the wine-shops and soaked themselves with liquor. Many a German from Mons to the Marne was drunk when he died or was made a prisoner.

When we had dashed through Coulommiers we had to halt, because the Germans had four batteries of guns and a division of cavalry waiting for us. So we retired to the cross-roads in the middle of the town, and had to take up almost exactly the same position as we did at Landrecies, where the Coldstreamers wiped out a strong German force in the street. We waited at Coulommiers till our heavy howitzer batteries were fetched up, then we lined the cross-roads, two howitzers were placed at the end of each street and we were in at the finish of the fight.

It was about midnight when the Germans started shelling us again, and the town blazed and boomed with the awful gunfire. We did not suffer much damage, but the houses were wrecked, and bricks and stones and pieces of timber were flying all about. A few of the bricks struck us, but we paid no heed to trifles like that. The Germans kept up the firing till about half-past two in the morning. Then, to our great surprise, they charged down the street.

"Lie still, boys, and let them come!" our officers shouted.

We lay perfectly quiet, and let the Germans rush on till they were almost upon us; then the sharp order came: "Ten rounds rapid fire!"

There was an absolute fusillade, and the ten rounds were fired in less than a minute, and simply struck the Germans down. Their dead and wounded were lying thick in the roadway and on the pavements when we sprang up and were after the survivors with the bayonet. This time we chased them up to the very muzzles of the guns, where we had a splendid bit of luck. The German gunners flew when they saw us, and we were on top of them and on top of the infantry. We dashed straight through the batteries, the enemy flying before the bayonet, and there, in the moonlight, which was almost as strong as daylight, I accounted for two of them with my own steel.

For fully three miles that furious chase was kept up, the Germans flying in all directions. It was a long and fierce fight in the moonlight, but at the end of it Coulommiers was ours, and six batteries of German guns and a thousand prisoners were ours, too, to say nothing of the killed and wounded.

You might have thought that enough had been done, but we had scarcely settled down to have a little drop of something hot to drink—and we needed it badly—when the cry arose, "Come on, boys; let's get after them again!" We emptied our canteens, which were full of hot coffee and rum, and were after the Germans again as hard as we could go. By daylight we had put the finish on them at Coulommiers. We were well pleased, too, with the fine haul of guns.

We had fought fiercely, and had not spared the Germans—no one could have any mercy on them who saw the proofs, as we had seen them, of their barbarities. When we advanced into Coulommiers we saw the bodies of two little girls who had been murdered and mutilated in a shocking manner. There were in that locality alone scores of such atrocities committed by the brutes who came from the land of "culture" and are being driven back to it.

I had a fair innings at the Marne, and saw a good deal of the beginning of the fight which started the Germans on the run. I had two days and nights of it; then I was bowled out by a piece of shell which struck me on the thigh and went off with a piece of flesh. I felt as if a brick had hit me, and when I saw the blood I thought it was all up with me. The doctor told me that this might easily have happened if the wound had been a little deeper. He was Lieutenant Huggin, of the Royal Army Medical Corps, a kind and brave gentleman, who was soon afterwards killed while doing his duty under fire. He was mentioned in despatches, with other officers who did so much. I remember one of them, a field officer of the Coldstreamers, during a very hot fight standing with his hands in his pockets watching to see how things were going, and saying, "Men, this is beautiful! We shall soon be on the other side of the river."

And we soon were—though to cross the Marne meant that we had at one time to fight waist deep in its waters.

The Battle of the Marne was hard, long work, following a long and terrible retreat; but it was a glorious victory. We had many privations, but also many compensations, and we were always cheerful, and very often singing. "Tipperary" was an easy first.

We often saw Sir John French and General Joffre, and I can tell you that when our own great field-marshal appeared it was as good as a victory for us, for we fairly worship him. Sir John is a thorough gentleman, and the friend of every soldier. He used to come into the trenches with his hands in his pockets and take no more notice of the German shells and bullets which were bursting and flying about than if they were peas shot by little boys.

One morning Sir John came round the trenches, and said, as usual, "Is everything all right, men?"

"Well, sir," he was told, "we want a drop of water, please." And we did want it, badly, because the weather was so fearfully hot, and we were almost boiled in our uniforms and heavy kits.

"Certainly; I'll see to that at once," replied the field-marshal. He immediately turned round, called to some men of the transport who were at hand, and told them to bring us some water at once.

General Joffre, too, was a great favourite. He speaks English well. Once when he came into the trenches he asked if there was anything we should like. Well, we wanted some cigarettes badly, and told him so, and he promptly took a box of about a hundred from his pocket, and handed them round. They went almost as fast as the Germans.

I am now well enough to be back at the front, and I'm keen to get into the firing line again, and rush along in some more bayonet charges—for those are the swoops that roll the Germans up as much as anything we do.

"Cavalry and guards got in amongst the Germans and fairly scattered them."

I have been a Coldstreamer for more than a dozen years, and have always been proud of it; but I never felt prouder than I do now, after reading what our great chief has said about us in despatches.

We have sometimes been called feather-bed soldiers; but we're known as "Coldsteelers" now, and try to live up to the reputation of our motto—"Second to none."

Chapter VII – An Armoured Car in Ambush

Trooper Stanley Dodds, Northumberland Hussars.

[Sir John French, in one of his despatches, expressed his great admiration of the splendid work which has been done at the front by our Territorials—that work, indeed, by this time has become almost equal to the glorious achievements of our Regular troops. The first of our Territorials to go into action during the war were the Northumberland Hussars, and this story is told by Trooper Stanley Dodds, of that fine corps, who was serving as a despatch-rider and on being wounded was invalided home. He afterwards returned to the front. Trooper Dodds is one of the best-known motor cyclists in the North, and winner in the competition of the summer of 1914 promoted by the North-Eastern Automobile Association. This was decided in North Yorkshire, over difficult country.]

I FANCY there are people in England who imagine that the life of a despatch-rider is one long unbroken joy ride. They seem to think that he gets somewhere near the front, and spends all his days careering over beautifully kept military roads between headquarters and the firing line, and seeing and enjoying everything that goes on; but I can assure such people that in practice despatch-riding does not work out like that at all.

I am only a humble member of the fraternity, but I have had a fair share of despatch work, and I do know that I have not had a single joy ride since I took the business on, and I can vouch for the fact that beautifully kept roads do not exist anywhere near the front, at any rate in Flanders. Even some of the so-called roads have never been roads—they were simply tracks to start with, and when military traffic had been going over them for some time they had lost all resemblance to roads, and you could scarcely tell the difference between them and the ordinary countryside.

The fact is that the life of a despatch-rider, though exciting enough to satisfy the cravings of any ordinary man, is largely an endless battle amongst bad roads, bullets and shell fire, want of sleep, and the hundred-and-one other things which often wreck the nerves; but the life is well worth living, all the same.

In work like this there is a good deal of nerve-racking riding and all sorts of difficult jobs have to be tackled. One of the worst I had to carry out while I was at the front was riding back to a patrol which was in our rear, and which had been lost sight of in the strain and turmoil of a rapid retirement.

The patrol had been left at a corner where there were some forked roads, and in order to reach them it was necessary to go through a village.

The Germans were everywhere and keenly on the look-out for a chance of sniping, so that there was plenty of excitement in the affair, especially as it was night and there was a darkness which was literally black.

This made the task doubly dangerous, for in addition to the ordinary risks of being shot there was the great danger of coming to serious grief on the road—a road which you could feel but scarcely see. I don't mind saying that when I started in the pitch darkness on this expedition I did not feel any too comfortable.

It is the custom at such times to ride without lights, because lights serve as targets, but in spite of this I was forced to light up, because it would have been utterly impossible to ride without some sort of guide.

After a good deal of trouble and a lot of risk I reached the village and then I had a most unpleasant shock, for a Belgian peasant told me that the Germans were actually occupying some of the houses.

That was a startling announcement, but the added danger forced me to set my wits to work to decide what it was best to do. At last I determined to make tracks down a side street.

I was riding very slowly and carefully when I was pulled up short with a sharp cry of "Halt" and I knew that a loaded rifle was covering me not far away.

I did halt—I didn't need to be told twice, not knowing what fate had in store for me; but thank heaven I quickly found that it was a British sentry who had spoken.

I rapidly told him what I was out to do, and I was very glad to have his help and advice.

The sentry told me that the patrol, like wise men, had acted on their own initiative and had fallen back on the village—and that was joyful news, because it meant that my work was practically done.

Being greatly relieved I could not resist the temptation to tell the sentry that I might have scooted past him and got clear, but my humour vanished when another British soldier from the darkness said grimly, "Yes, you might have got past *him*, but *I* should have put a bullet into you!"

I have not the slightest doubt that this smart fellow spoke the truth—anyway, if he had missed me I should doubtless have been potted by a chum of his, because there were four sentries posted at short distances from this place. I could not see a sign of them, but of course they had my light as a target and they were as keen as mustard, knowing that the Germans were in the village.

There were a good many little thrilling experiences for all of us which came in as part of the day's work, and most of them were thoroughly enjoyable—a few in particular I would not have missed for worlds. One of these was a little jaunt with an armoured motor-car.

Incidentally, this experience showed me that we have learnt a good deal from the South African War. It is pretty common knowledge by this time that the Germans sprang something of a surprise on the world with their big guns; but our own armoured cars came on the Germans with even more stunning effect. It was the South African War which to a great extent gave us the most useful knowledge we now possess of armoured cars and armoured trains.

The armoured car is a development of the idea of the armoured train, with this enormous advantage, that you can get your car pretty nearly anywhere, while the train is limited in its operations to the lines on which it runs. Remarkably good motor-car work at the front has been done by Brigadier-General Seely and Commander Sampson. Some of these cars are extremely powerful and fast, with huge wheels, and in the hands of skilful drivers they can overcome almost any obstacle.

In order to meet the exceptional demands which a war like this makes upon them the cars have to be specially protected and strengthened. The body itself is protected with toughened steel, which has so much resistance that bullets simply make no impression on it, and light guns can therefore be mounted behind the metal which can do enormous execution amongst bodies of the enemy's riflemen or troops who are not protected by anything but rifles. If you want excitement, therefore, you can get it to the full by being associated with these machines. Whenever they go out they simply look for trouble—and they can afford to do so, because they despise ordinary cavalry and infantry tactics. Their chief gain has been Uhlan patrols, which they have wiped out with the greatest ease.

Scouts bring in word of enemy patrols on the road; off swoop the cars straight to the spot, and the fun begins.

My own little job was not actually in an armoured car, but accompanying one. Very often, in the case of a retreat, the cars remain behind the main line, to do the work of wiping out as many of the enemy's advanced guards as they can get under fire, and an affair of this description took place during the retreat from Roulers.

I happened to be there, armed with my rifle, which I carry in preference to a revolver, because I have found it more useful.

I stayed behind to keep in touch with the armoured car. This was at a corner of one of the roads, and a prominent feature of the district was a brewery, the entrance to which commanded the approach by road.

Matters at that particular time were very lively and the car was swiftly run into the yard, where with astonishing skill and speed it was disguised as much as possible and then it was ready to give the Germans a surprise.

I left my machine round the corner, and made my way into one of the nearest of the houses. Rushing upstairs, I entered a bedroom and went to the window, where I took up a position with my rifle, and kept properly on the alert, for you never knew from which quarter a bullet would come and settle your account for ever.

There was every reason to believe that the enemy would come—and they did. They came along as if they were satisfied that nothing could happen to them—certainly the German body that was making its way along the road had no idea that a disguised motor-car was ready to give it a welcome as soon as it got within striking distance of the entrance to the brewery. Being Germans, doubtless their thoughts, when they saw the brewery, were more concentrated on beer than on the British troops in ambush.

On the Germans came, and one could not help feeling how awful it was that they should be advancing utterly unsuspectingly into a perfect death-trap.

From behind my bedroom window, rifle in hand, I watched them come up to their doom. They got nearer and nearer to the innocent-looking brewery entrance and to the houses and other places where the unseen rifles were covering them; then, just at the right moment, the maxims from the armoured car rattled and the rifles kept them company.

The German ranks were shattered and scattered instantly. It was a swift and destructive cannonade and the Germans went down in the fatal roadway just like ninepins. I do not think I exaggerate when I say that practically the whole of the enemy's advanced guard was wiped out in a few moments.

This little affair was as short as it was brilliant and decisive, and almost before there was time to realise fully what had happened the car was stripped of its disguise and was triumphantly driven out of the brewery yard and back to the British lines.

When I saw the car going I took it as a signal that I had better make tracks myself, so I hurried away from the bedroom, got clear of the house, jumped on to my machine, and lost no time in following it.

This fine performance, typical of a great number of such deeds done in the war by resourceful men of which nothing has been heard and perhaps never will be, strikes me as being a very good illustration of doing exactly those things which the enemy does not expect you to do. Personally, I have always made a point of putting this principle into practice. If the enemy is waiting for you to take the highroad, the obvious thing, it seems to me, is to take to the fields, especially as in bad weather, in a country like Flanders, there is very little difference between the fields and the roads.

There is one interesting point which I may mention, and it is that so far I have had no difficulty in finding petrol. Nearly all the Belgian farmers use gas-engines, and their stores are very useful for motor cycles. I need hardly say that I never saw any want of willingness on the part of Belgian farmers to help the fighters who are doing their best to get the country back for them.

At present I am not a bit useful as a fighting man, because when I was going into the trenches I heard the ping of a German bullet and found that blood was running down my arm.

When I was actually struck I felt only a numb sensation, and did not for some time know what had happened; but later it was discovered that the bullet had struck me between the wrist and elbow of the right arm and had gone clean through, leaving a hole on each side of the arm.

Strange though it may seem, I felt little pain at any time, in spite of the fact that one of the bones of the arm was broken, and I am glad to say that this wound—and there have been an enormous number like it since the war began—

is making a first-class recovery, and I shall soon be all right again.

A man does not go to war for fun, but there is a bright side to the grim business, as I found when I reached a Belgian hospital. I spent three very comfortable days there, and when I was sent off to England the nurse who was attending me very gravely made me a little present, which I as gravely accepted. She paid me three-halfpence! I did not know what it meant, but I concluded that I had received the Belgian's rate of daily pay as a soldier, and his keep. I was perfectly satisfied, and I hope my excellent nurse was the same.

An armoured Rolls-Royce car of the period - Image: Hohum

Chapter VIII – Exploits of the London Scottish

Private J. E. Carr, 14th (County of London) Battalion London Regiment (London Scottish).

["Eye-Witness," in his descriptive account of November 4th, dealing with the first phase of the desperate fight for Ypres, said that a special feature of the battle was that it formed an epoch in the military history of the British Empire, and marked the first time that a complete unit of our Territorial Army has been thrown into the fight alongside its sister units of the Regulars. That unit was the 14th (County of London) Battalion London Regiment, better known as the London Scottish. Its ranks contained many prominent men who gave up everything at their country's call and went to the front. Amongst them was Mr. J. E. Carr, Managing Director of Scremerston Colliery, Northumberland, a well-known breeder of Border Leicester sheep, a keen rider to hounds and a thoroughly good sportsman. Private Carr served with the London Scottish until he was wounded and invalided home and it is his story which is here retold.\]

IT is very difficult to keep within defined limits the varied experiences that are crowded into a few months at the front in a war which is waged on such a vast scale as the present conflict. Every day has its own fresh and particular excitements which are worth remembering, and one can scarcely pick out, off-hand, the most startling or interesting phases of the campaigning. However, the earliest impressions undoubtedly cling most tenaciously, and I have vivid recollections of the thrill I experienced when our transport swung to her moorings and the London Scottish disembarked on the other side of the Channel.

I should like to say here that the London Scottish have been the subject of a good deal of comment, mostly favourable, I am glad to know; but there has been undue exaltation. The blame for this certainly does not rest with the

London Scottish, but in other perfectly well-meaning quarters.

I am proud indeed to belong to the London Scottish, because they are good boys to be amongst, so good that there was no reason whatever why people should have expressed surprise that the first Territorials to go into action did so well. I don't think there was any reason for astonishment, for the London Scottish had been a well-trained body of Volunteers before the Territorial system came into being. And if they pulled through, as they did, when the actual fighting began, do not let it be forgotten that they had some glorious examples to follow. On their left and on their right were some of the very finest soldiers in the world, and it was for the London Scottish to prove that they were worthy of fighting with these truly splendid fellows. Troops like the Coldstream Guards, the Scots Guards, the Black Watch and the Cameron Highlanders are men with whom it is indeed an honour to be associated.

Our landing on the Continent was an event which I shall remember all my life. It meant that we were many miles nearer to the band of heroes who had held the Germans up at Mons and had completely disarranged a whole plan of campaign. Whenever I meet a man who fought in that greatest of rearguard actions I want to take off my hat to him.

It was not long after the war began that we found ourselves on the lines of communication and began to feel that we were really bearing a hand in the things that mattered. This was in September, and the weather being good we found it no great hardship to guard railways, escort prisoners, run up ammunition for the fighting lines and do any odd job that came along. There was not a man amongst us who did not put his back into the business, realising that it was all a part of the tremendous game that was being played, monotonous and unexciting though the duties might be, and with every day that passed we got fitter and keener and better able to meet the heavy calls that came upon us later. We felt that we were really "in" and part of the great adventure. In various ways we did a good deal of wandering, and some of us went as far south as Nantes.

This was about harvest time, and we saw the old men of France and the women and the boys gathering in the sheaves. Later on we saw even the women ploughing, and very good work they did. One thing which particularly astonished us was their courage in working on the land quite close up to the fighting line. They were often well within shell fire, but they did not seem to be in the least disturbed. I suppose they thought that if their husbands and sons and brothers could fight for France at rifle and bayonet range they could go on working for their country in spite of a stray shell or two.

A few weeks later we moved up to the firing line, and then we had the opportunity of seeing how gloriously the Scottish Regular troops were doing their work and maintaining the splendid traditions of the Highland regiments.

People have become so used to amazing happenings in this war that it is not easy to realise that only a very few months ago the mere sight of an aeroplane was a novelty, and it was a thrill indeed for us when, near Béthune, we had a splendid view of a fight in the air between British, French and German airmen. The German, in a machine which looked exactly like an enormous bird in the sky, came scouting over our lines, to find out what was going on. The mere sight of him was enough to fetch along a British 'plane and a Frenchman followed. This happened on a clear, peaceful Sunday morning, and it was truly wonderful to see how the three machines were manœuvred to get the top position and so spell doom to the lowest 'plane. By extraordinary daring and skill, and because his very life hung in the balance, the German managed to get away, in spite of the most desperate efforts of his opponents to bag him. But I don't think he would escape to-day, when the British and French airmen have so fully established their superiority over the German flyers and when it has been proved that the machines of the

Allies are far better than any of the craft that the German airmen use.

One of our first experiences of real fighting came when we were ordered to charge at Messines. I do not care to say much about that charge, because I think too much has been said of it already; so I will not go beyond saying that it was hot and sanguinary work with the bayonet and that we lost many good fellows. I cannot help thinking that the London Scottish got too much praise for Messines, and they are the first to admit that; but this was due to the fact that correspondents and others spread themselves out on the charge and gave special attention to the matter because of the fact that up to that time practically nothing had been heard of Territorials in action.

The praise that was given to the regiment had the effect of making us rather unpopular with the Regulars, and naturally enough, too, seeing that they had been constantly doing the same sort of work ever since the beginning of the war. It was pride enough for us to be in the same brigade as the Coldstreamers, the Scots Guards, the Black Watch and the Camerons, and to feel that we had done just what we were told to do. It was, of course, a source of great satisfaction to us afterwards to be congratulated by General Munro on what he was good enough to term our "steadiness as a battalion." Now that is all I am going to say about the charge of the London Scottish at Messines.

Speaking generally the fighting from November until the time I was wounded can be divided into two distinct parts, the actions around Ypres and the affairs at La Bassée. At Ypres about fifty men of our regiment were in the city during the siege, and a very exciting time we had. Shells were constantly bursting all around and no matter where the people were they did not seem to be able to keep clear of danger. Even the cellars, in which large numbers of men and women and children sought refuge, were at times blown in and there were some very distressing and unpleasant sights. Personally, I was uncommonly lucky, because I escaped being hurt.

I had the good fortune to sleep for two nights in the beautiful and famous Cloth Hall, of which the story is told that it was particularly spared by the German artillery because the Kaiser meant to enter it in state at the head of his victorious troops. But when I was in it the shells came pounding on the walls and roof of the hall, doing grievous damage, though our own men had the good luck to escape. Not so lucky were some men of the Suffolk Regiment who followed us, for one afternoon a huge shell came through and burst and killed five of the Suffolks and wounded a number of other men of that fine regiment.

So much has been said of the enormous German shells which have become known as Jack Johnsons that people have almost ceased to be affected by their performances; but nothing that I have heard or read conveys any real idea of the extraordinarily destructive nature of these awful engines of war when they explode—and that, luckily, does not always happen. One afternoon, however, we counted no fewer than thirty of them which *did* explode, and the results were absolutely devastating.

When the Germans really set to work to bombard Ypres, the Cloth Hall and the splendid cathedral were soon practically destroyed; but one of the most noticeable things in connection with this destruction was that many sacred objects were undamaged whilst there was ruin all around them. Take the case of the crucifix of Ypres Cathedral—it is literally true that this was found entire and upright amongst such general ruin that it seemed as if only a miracle could have saved it. In several other places I saw crucifixes hanging uninjured on walls of houses although the structures themselves had been practically wrecked. On the other hand, while we were in the trenches I saw a little nickel crucifix with a bullet-hole right through it.

With the King's Royal Rifles on their right, and fired by their glorious example, the London Scottish were in some furious fighting in the earlier days of November, and the coming of Christmas brought more hot work. On December 22nd we marched about twenty-six miles with the brigade, and the Coldstreamers, gallant as ever, went straight into action after their arrival. They did fine work that day, and paid for it accordingly. There followed a rest at Béthune and then we went into more trouble in the neighbourhood of Givenchy.

Very little of what may be called spectacular fighting was seen hereabouts; it was mostly trench work, and this was all the more difficult because the German trenches were so close to our own, and the real old-fashioned way of conducting a battle was out of the question. But all the same we got some variations, and one of these was a fight for a brick-field which was a good hot performance while it lasted.

At this period we made a change on the usual form of trench by lining our own trenches with bricks, which were handy for the purpose. These trenches were more comfortable than the general type, but they were more dangerous, because when a shell burst near us the bricks splintered, so that the flying bricks had to be added to the dangers and discomforts of the flying metal fragments.

One of the brick splinters struck my hand and poisoned it, and another unwelcome attention that was paid to me was a piece of shrapnel in the back of the neck; but these were really very minor details compared with the injuries that were received by other members of the London Scottish, and I am not for a moment complaining, nor can I, for when I came home my company had only twenty left out of 119. There had been the casualties in the charge and in other affairs, and a number of men had been killed and wounded in the trenches.

At Givenchy we had to endure as best we could that most unpleasant engine of war which is called the trench mortar. This affects high-angle fire and plumps a shell into the trenches when the aim is good. One shell dropped into a trench of ours and exploded, killing one man and wounding five others—a round half-dozen fine fellows as toll to a single German shot.

There were the snipers, too, pests who are intensely disliked by the British soldier. These fellows find a lodging in what seems to be an impossible sort of place, often enough high up a tree, and being well supplied with food and ammunition they can go on potting for a long time without going down from their perch. It was always matter for rejoicing when one of these queer birds was winged.

I spent Christmas in the trenches, with the boys. It is odd to be talking about Christmas at this time of the year, but that season was an outstanding feature of the experiences of the London Scottish, just as the New Year was. Christmas Day was comparatively comfortable because there was a lull in the fighting. New Year's Day was unforgettable to those who saw it in and did their best to keep up the national custom.

I think that of all the strange incidents that have been recorded in connection with this war, and they have been many—and some of them have proved how soon soldiers become impervious to the most terrible happenings of campaigning—one of the strangest must have been the sight we saw on New Year's Eve.

When the New Year actually came in we fired three rounds rapid, and the pipes of the Black Watch rose on the night, while our own voices broke into "Auld lang syne." Wonderful and affecting it was to hear the pipes and the dear old tune and many of us were deeply moved.

The effect on the Germans was very curious. Apparently they judged from the sounds of the pipes and the roll of the song that the Scots were going to pay them a special visit with the bayonet, and by way of being ready for it and giving us a welcome, they sent up star-lights, and these, bursting in the air, gave a sinister illumination of the landscape and would have shown us up if we had had in mind the purpose of an assault on the German trenches. But we had no intention of letting the New Year in upon them in such an unfriendly manner, although later in the day we were of necessity hard at it again in the ordinary way of firing.

From day to day the London Scottish kept at it, doing their best, I hope; then, on January 25th a spell of uncommonly hard work came along. The Coldstreamers, who had held out gloriously and successfully against great odds, had to withdraw from their trenches owing to an overwhelming attack by the enemy. For the time being the Germans had scored and no doubt they were exulting in their best manner, but the London Scottish were sent up to reinforce the Coldstreamers—and proud they were to do it. Later in the afternoon the Black Watch, with the Sussex Regiment and the Royal Rifles, came up too, and the combination proved too much for the Germans, who, after a brilliant attack, were sent flying back to their own trenches.

I have heard that many old and young Germans have been taken prisoners at various parts of the immense battle-front of the Allies; but those that I saw pass through our lines were neither very old nor very young. Occasionally we observed signs that they required a good lot of leading, that is to say, "leading" from behind; but generally speaking they seemed to be the best men that Germany had and on the whole they were undoubtedly good fighters.

While talking of German prisoners I am reminded of a particularly ugly incident. When I was taken to the hospital I was with a number of German prisoners.

The hospital rule is that everything shall be taken away from the patient until the time comes for him to be discharged. Well, when one of these prisoners was searched I learned to my amazement, disgust and anger, that he carried with him a bomb which was powerful enough to blow up the whole place—but prompt steps were taken to prevent him from making any use of it. How on earth he had got so far from the lines with the deadly thing I cannot understand; but he had it with him all right.

We got a good deal of amusement and help from a new set of "Ten Commandments for Soldiers in the Field," which were duly but not officially published. I will quote one or two by way of showing their character and indicating that incorrigible British cheerfulness which the German, with all his "culture," cannot understand. Number Three ran: "Thou shalt not use profane language except under extraordinary circumstances, such as seeing thy comrade shot or getting petrol in thy tea." Number Four was worded: "Remember that the soldier's week consists of seven days. Six days shalt thou labour and do all thy work, and on the seventh do all thy odd jobs!" "Honour thy King and country," was the Fifth. "Keep thy rifle oiled, and shoot straight, in order that thy days may be long upon the land the enemy giveth thee." Then we had, "Thou shalt not steal thy neighbour's kit," and "Thou shalt not kill—time!" By Number Nine it was enjoined, "Thou shalt not bear false witness against thy comrade, but preserve discreet silence on his outgoings and incomings." Last of all came Number Ten, full of a wonderful hope for the lowly: "Thou shalt not covet thy Sergeant's post, nor the Corporal's, nor the Staff-Major's, but do thy duty and by dint of perseverance rise to the high position of Field-Marshal."

(This is one of the first detailed stories to be told of some of the achievements of the London Scottish at the front, and its modest vein is in keeping with the general point of view of the members of this distinguished corps. It has been for others, not of the London Scottish, to tell us something of what the regiment really did at Messines and elsewhere in those early days of the Ypres fighting on which such vast issues depended. What happened at Messines was this: The regiment was in reserve when unexpectedly the order came to hurry up to the support of the hard-pressed Regular troops, who were being fiercely assailed by very much superior German forces. Crowding on to motor-buses the London Scottish were hurried along in the course of the afternoon and while some of them spent the night in deserted cottages others bivouacked in the streets, waiting for daylight.

After much marching and wandering, the zone of fire was entered, and the fine battalion which not many weeks before had marched along London streets after being embodied made acquaintance with the German shells and got ready to show what the British Territorials could do with the rifle and the bayonet.

The regiment was amused and interested in the antics of a windmill the sails of which turned constantly and oddly, although there was no wind. It was not until later that the phenomenon was explained and that was when the windmill was visited and a German spy was caught in the act of signalling, by means of the sails, the position and movements of the British troops.

It was at Hollebecke and at Messines, between Ypres and Warneton, that the British lines were hard pressed owing to the determined attempts of the Germans to break through and hack their way to Calais, and it was here that the London Scottish went to support the Cavalry Brigade who were holding the trenches.

Forming up under the crest of a hill they advanced over the crest and found themselves right in the battle line. Hurrying down the slope, struggling over heavy ground which was made all the harder because of beet crops, the regiment went into a most destructive artillery and rifle and machine-gun fire.

Many a splendid fellow was shot down before he could use his own rifle, and others were wounded; but nothing could stop the advance. By short rushes, and taking cover, the men in time reached the trenches and had to encounter an overwhelming assault of Germans with the bayonet.

Now it was that a wonderful and splendid thing was done, for these Territorials, fresh from civil life, hurled themselves with the bayonet upon the finest troops of Germany. They were thrown back. Again they charged, only to be driven off once more; but the regiment was not to be denied or beaten and with a final furious rush the Germans were scattered and the day was won for the British. No wonder that Colonel J. H. Scott, late of the Gordon Highlanders and formerly adjutant of the London Scottish, wrote on hearing the glorious news: "Hurrah for the London Scottish! From my knowledge of them I knew they would do it!")

Chapter IX – The Rout of the Prussian Guard at Ypres

Private H. J. Polley, 2nd Battalion Bedfordshire Regiment.

[The official writers have told us of the almost superhuman efforts made by the Germans to break through to Calais so that they might, from that place, either raid or bombard England. For a whole month a little British army round Ypres held its ground against the repeated onslaughts of overwhelming German hosts. These actions were divided into two phases, the first lasting from October 20th to November 2nd, and the second from November 3rd to 17th. German infantry of the Line having failed to win success, the vaunted Prussian Guard was hurried up, and, encouraged by the presence of the braggart Most High War Lord himself, hurled itself in frenzy against the British troops, only to be thrown back and broken. This crushing of the crack corps of Prussia was a bitter blow to the Kaiser and the German people, who believed it to be invincible. In these unexampled contests the Glorious Seventh Infantry Division bore the brunt of battle, and the tale of the first phase is told by Private H. J. Polley, 2nd Battalion Bedfordshire Regiment. Lieutenant-General Sir H. S. Rawlinson, commanding the Division, said in an order: "You have been called to take a conspicuous part in one of the severest struggles of the war.... The Seventh Division has gained for itself a reputation for stubborn valour and endurance in defence." When the Glorious Seventh was withdrawn from the firing line only forty-four officers were left out of 400 who had sailed from England, and only 2,336 out of 12,000 men.]

ALL the world knows now how furiously the Germans tried to hack their way through to Calais, so that they could have their fling at the hated English. It is known too that they were held and hurled back.

I am going to tell you something of the way in which this was done, for I belong to the Bedfordshire Regiment, the old 16th Foot, and the Bedfords were part of the Glorious Seventh Division, and did their share in keeping back the German forces, which included the Prussian Guards, the Kaiser's pet men. They had been rushed up to this position because it was thought that no troops could stand against them.

These idols of the German nation are picked men and brave fellows, and at that time had an absolute belief in their own invincibility; but events proved that they were no match for the British Guards and the rest of the British troops who fought them at Ypres, and practically wiped them out. I saw these Prussian Guards from Berlin mown down by our artillery, machine-gun and rifle fire, and I saw them lying dead in solid masses—walls of corpses.

The Kaiser had planned to enter Ypres as a conqueror, at the head of his Guards; but he hurried off a beaten man, leaving his slaughtered Guards in heaps.

Originally in the 1st Battalion of the Bedfords, I later went into the 2nd, and I was serving with the 2nd in South Africa when the European War broke out. It is an interesting fact that nearly all the battalions which formed the Seventh Division came from foreign service—India, Egypt, Africa and elsewhere—which meant that many of the men of the Seventh had seen active service and were veteran fighters. They had not learned their warfare at peace manœuvres in Germany. Our Division consisted of the 1st Grenadier Guards, the 2nd Scots Guards, the 2nd Border, 2nd Gordon Highlanders, 2nd Bedfordshire, 2nd Yorkshire, 2nd Royal Scots Fusiliers, 2nd Wiltshire, 2nd Royal West Surrey, 2nd Royal Warwickshire, 1st Royal Welsh Fusiliers, 1st South Staffordshire, and the Northumberland Hussars; and we had a pom-pom detachment and horse, field and garrison artillery. We were under Major-General Sir T. Capper, D.S.O.

We had been sent to help the Naval Division at Antwerp, and early in October we landed at Zeebrugge—the only division to land at that port. But we were not there long, for we soon learned that we were too late, and that Antwerp had fallen. We were sorry, but there was no time for moping, and we were quickly on the move to the quaint old city of Bruges, where we were billeted for a night. Sir Harry Rawlinson had moved his headquarters from Bruges to Ostend, so next day we marched towards Ostend and took up outpost. Then we had a forced march back to Bruges, and from Bruges we started marching, but we did not know where we were going till we got to the city of Ypres.

So far we had not had any fighting. We had been marching and marching, first to one place, then to another, constantly expecting to come into action, and very nearly doing so, for the Germans were swarming all over the countryside. We had to be content with being on outpost and guarding bridges, and so on—hard and necessary work, we knew; but we wanted something more thrilling, something bigger—and we eventually got it.

There was practically only the Seventh Division available for anything that turned up. The Northumberland Hussars were able to give a very good account of themselves, and were, I believe, the first Yeomanry corps to go into action. The few Uhlans I saw while I was at the front had been taken prisoners by these Hussars, who brought them in, lances and all. But there is very little to say about cavalry work; it was mostly a matter for the infantry, and, of course, the artillery—the wonderful British gunners who have punished the Germans so severely whenever they have met them.

While we were around Ypres, waiting for the Germans to come and break through, we heard a good deal, indirectly, of what was going to happen to us and to England. The Germans had all sorts of monster guns, and with these they were going to bombard England across the narrow Channel when they got to the French coast, and they were going to work all sorts of miracles with their airships and aeroplanes.

We soon heard, too, that the Kaiser himself was in the field; but the only effect of that information was to make us more keen to show what we could do. Truth to tell, we were far from being impressed by the presence of either the Kaiser or his vaunted Guards. We were in the best of spirits, and had a sublime belief in Sir John French and all his staff and our own officers.

It was on October 31st—which has been called *the* decisive day of the fight for Ypres, and which was certainly a most terrible day in every way—that the Seventh Division was ordered to attack the German position. The weather was very fine, clear and sunny, and our spirits were in keeping with it. We were thankful to be on the move, because we had had nearly three weeks in the trenches, and had been billeted in all sorts of queer places—above and below ground—under an everlasting shell fire, which became unendurable and was thoroughly nerve-destroying.

We knew what a desperate business the advance would be, because the Germans greatly outnumbered us, and they had planted vast numbers of guns. They had immense bodies of men in trenches, and in a large number of the houses and buildings which commanded the ground over which we had to advance they had placed machine-guns, with their villainous muzzles directed on us from bedroom windows and holes which had been knocked in walls.

From start to finish the advance was a terrible business—far more terrible than any words of mine can make you realise. The whole Division was on the move, stretching along a big tract of country; but of course no man could see much of what was happening, except in his own immediate locality. Neither had he much chance of thinking about anything or anybody except himself, and then only in a numbed sort of way, because of the appalling din of the artillery on both sides, the crash of the guns and the explosions of the shells, with the ceaseless rattle of the rifles and the machine-guns.

At the beginning, the regiments kept fairly well together, but very soon we were all mixed up, and you could not tell what regiment a man belonged to, unless he wore a kilt; then you knew that, at any rate, he wasn't a Bedford. Some of us had our packs and full equipment. Others were without packs, having been compelled to throw them away. But there was not a man who had let his rifle go: that is the last thing of all to be parted from; it is the soldier's very life. And every man had a big supply of ammunition, with plenty in reserve. The general himself took part in the advance, and what he did was done by every other officer present. There was no difference between officer and man, and a thing to be specially noticed is the fact that the officers got hold of rifles and blazed away as hard as any man.

Never, during the whole of the war, had there been a more awful fire than that which we gave the Germans. Whenever we got the chance, we gave them what they call the "Englishman's mad minute"—that is, the dreadful fifteen rounds a minute rapid fire. We drove it into them and mowed them down. Many a soldier, when his own rifle was too hot to hold, threw it down and snatched the rifle of a dead or wounded comrade who had no further use for it, and with this fresh, cool weapon he continued the deadly work by which success could alone be won. I do not know what the German losses were, but I do know that I saw bodies lying around in solid masses, while we passed our own dead and wounded everywhere as we advanced. Where they fell they had to stay; it was impossible to do anything for them while the fighting continued.

The whole of the advance consisted of a series of what might be called ups and downs—a little rush, then a "bob down." At most, no one rush carried us more than fifty yards; then we dropped out of sight as best we could, to get a breather and prepare for another dash. It was pretty open country hereabouts, so that we were fully exposed to the German artillery and rifle fire, in addition to the hail from the machine-guns in the neighbouring buildings. Here and there we found little woods and clumps of trees and bits of rising ground and ditches and hedges—and you may take it from me that shelter of any sort was very welcome and freely used.

A remarkable feature of this striving to hide from the enemy's fire was that it was almost impossible to escape from the shells and bullets for any appreciable time, for the simple reason that the Germans altered their range in the most wonderful manner. So surely as we got the shelter of a little wood or ditch, they seemed to have the distance almost instantly, and the range was so accurate that many a copse and ditch became a little graveyard in the course of that advance.

At one point as we went along I noticed a small ditch against a hedge. It was a dirty, uninviting ditch, deep in water; but it seemed to offer promising shelter, and so some officers and men made a rush for it, meaning to take cover. They had no sooner scrambled into the ditch and were thinking themselves comparatively safe than the Germans got the range of them with machine-guns, and nearly the whole lot were annihilated. In this case, as in others, the enemy had been marvellously quick with their weapons, and had swept the ditch with bullets. I don't know what happened to the fine fellows who had fallen. We had to leave them and continue the advance.

The forenoon passed, noon came, and the afternoon was with us; still the fighting went on, the guns on both sides crashing without cessation, and the machine-guns and the rifles rattling on without a break. The air was filled with screaming, bursting shells and whistling bullets, and the ground was ploughed and torn everywhere. It was horrible beyond expression, yet it fired the blood in us, so that the only thing that mattered was to put the finish to the work, get up to the Germans, and rout them out of their positions.

At last, after endless spells of lying down and jumping up, we got near enough to make it possible to charge, and the order went round to get ready. We now saw what big, fine fellows we had to tackle. Clearly now we could distinguish the Prussian Guards, and a thing that particularly struck me just then was that their bayonets looked very cruel. The Guards wore cloth-covered brass helmets, and through the cloth we could see the gleam of the brass in the sunshine.

The nearer we got, the more clearly we saw what splendid chaps they were, and what a desperate business it would be when we actually reached the long, snaky blades of steel—much longer than our own bayonets—with longer rifles, too, so that the Germans had the pull of us in every way. But all that counted as nothing, and there was not a man amongst us who was not hungering to be in amongst them.

The order to fix bayonets came quietly, and it was carried out without any fuss whatever, just as a part of the day's work. We were lying down when the order came, and as we lay we got round at our bayonets, drew them and fixed them, and I could hear the rattle of the fixing all along the line, just as I had heard it many times on parade or at manœuvres—the same sound, but with what a different purpose!

A few of the fellows did not fix their bayonets as we lay, but they managed to do it as we ran, when we had jumped up and started to rush along to put the finish to the fight. There was no bugle sound, we just got the word to charge, an order which was given to the whole of the Seventh Division.

When this last part of the advance arrived we started halloaing and shouting, and the Division simply hurled itself against the Prussian Guard. By the time we were up with the enemy we were mad. I can't tell you much of what actually happened—and I don't think any man who took part in it could do so—but I do know that we rushed helter-skelter, and that when we got up to the famous Guards there were only two of my own section holding together—Lance-Corporal Perry and myself, and even we were parted immediately afterwards.

The next thing I clearly knew was that we were actually on the Prussians, and that there was some very fierce work going on. There was some terrific and deadly scrimmaging, and whatever the Prussian Guard did in the way of handling the steel, the Seventh Division did better.

It was every man for himself. I had rushed up with the rest, and the first thing I clearly knew was that a tremendous Prussian was making at me with his villainous bayonet. I made a lunge at him as hard and swift as I could, and he did the same to me. I thought I had him, but I just missed, and as I did so, I saw his own long, ugly blade driven out at the end of his rifle. Before I could do anything to parry the thrust, the tip of the bayonet had ripped across my right thigh, and I honestly thought that it was all up with me.

Then, when I reckoned that my account was paid, when I supposed that the huge Prussian had it all his own way, one of our chaps—I don't know who, I don't suppose I ever shall; but I bless him—rushed up, drove his bayonet into the Prussian and settled him. I am sure that if this had not been done I should have been killed by the Prussian; as it was, I was able to get away without much inconvenience at the end of the bayonet fight.

This struggle lasted about half-an-hour, and fierce, hard work it was all the time. In the end we drove the Guards away and sent them flying—all except those who had fallen; the trench was full of the latter, and we took no prisoners. Then we were forced to retire ourselves, for the ample reason that we were not strong enough to hold the position that we had taken at such a heavy cost. The enemy did not know it then, though perhaps they found out later, that we had nicely deceived them in making them believe that we had reinforcements. But we had nothing of the sort; yet we had stormed and taken the position and driven its defenders away.

We were far too weak to hold the position, and so we retired over the ground that we had won, getting back a great deal faster than we had advanced. We had spent the best part of the day in advancing and reaching the enemy's position; and it seemed as if we must have covered a great tract of country, but as a matter of fact we had advanced less than a mile. It had taken us many hours to cover that short distance; but along the whole of the long line of the advance the ground was littered with the fallen—the officers and men who had gone down under such a storm of shells and bullets as had not been known since the war began.

Retiring, we took up a position behind a wood, and were thinking that we should get a bit of a rest, when a German aeroplane came flying over us, gave our hiding-place away, and brought upon us a fire that drove us out and sent us back to three lines of trenches which we had been occupying.

"I made a lunge at him, but just missed, and I saw his own long, ugly blade driven out."

By this time our ambulances were hard at work; but ambulance or no ambulance, the pitiless shelling went on, and I saw many instances of German brutality in this respect. The ambulance vehicles were crowded, and I saw one which had two wounded men standing on the back, because there was not room enough for them inside. Shells were bursting all around, and a piece struck one of the poor chaps and took part of his foot clean away. He instantly fell on to the road, and there he had to be left. I hope he got picked up by another ambulance, though I doubt it, for the shell-firing just then was heavy, and deliberately aimed at helpless ambulances by people who preach what they call culture!

We made the best of things during the evening and the night in the trenches. The next day things were reversed, for the Germans came on against us; but we kept up a furious fight, and simply mowed them down as they threw themselves upon us. We used to say, "Here comes another bunch of 'em!" and then we gave them the "mad minute." We had suffered heavily on the 31st, and we were to pay a big bill again on this 1st of November, amongst our casualties being two of our senior officers.

The battalion was in the peculiar position of having no colonel at the head of it, our commanding officer being Major J. M. Traill. I should like to say now, by way of showing how heavily the Bedfords suffered, that in one of Sir John French's despatches, published early in the year, seven officers were mentioned, and in the cases of six of them it had to be added that they had been killed in action. Major Traill and Major R. P. Stares were killed not far from me on the day I am telling of—and within two hours of each other.

We were lying in trenches, and the majors were in front of us, walking about, and particularly warning us to be careful and not expose ourselves. Their first thought seemed to be for us, and their last for themselves.

Just at that time there was some uncommonly deadly sniping going on, and any figure that was seen even for a fraction of time was a certain target. The sniper himself was a specially chosen German, and he had as a companion and look-out a smart chap with field-glasses, to sweep the countryside and report to the sniper anything promising that he saw in the way of a target. Working in pairs like this, the snipers were able to pick off the two majors as they walked up and down directing and encouraging us. They were shot, and, as far as we could tell, killed instantly. We felt their loss very greatly.

Major Stares had very much endeared himself to his men, and he was a great favourite in South Africa before the war began. We were all eager to get to the front, of course, and were constantly talking about what we should do, and wondering what would happen when we met the Germans.

The major was never tired of explaining what we ought to do in tight and dangerous corners, and asking us what *we* should do. I have known him stop us in the street to ask us these questions, so keen and anxious was he for our welfare.

The second day of the fighting passed and the third came. Still we held on, but it became clear that we were too hopelessly outnumbered to hope for complete success at the time, and so we were forced to leave the trenches. Withdrawing again, we took up positions in farmhouses and woods and any other places that gave shelter. All the time there was a killing fire upon us, and it happened that entire bodies of men would be wiped out in a few moments. A party of the Warwicks got into a wood near us, and they had no sooner taken shelter than the German gunners got the range of them, shelled them, and killed nearly all of them.

There was not a regiment of the Glorious Seventh that had not suffered terribly in the advance during the three days' fateful fighting. The Bedfords had lost, all told, about 600, and it was a mere skeleton of the battalion that formed up when the roll was called. But there was one pleasant surprise for me, and that was meeting again with Lance-Corporal Perry. We had lost sight of each other in the hand-to-hand fighting with the Prussian Guard, and met again when we were reorganised at an old château; and very thankful we were to compare notes, especially as each of us thought that the other was a dead man. There were a good many cases of soldiers turning up who were supposed to be either killed or wounded, or, what is worse, missing. In the inevitable disorder and confusion of such a battle they had got separated from their own regiments and had joined others; but they turned up in due course in their right places.

I had become a member of the grenade company of the battalion, which was something like going back to the early days of the Army, when the grenadier companies of the regiments flung their little bombs at the enemy. So did we, and grim work it was, hurling home-made bombs, which had the power of doing a great amount of mischief.

I was with the grenade company, behind a brick wall close to the trenches, and was sitting with several others round a fire which we had made in a biscuit-tin. We were quite a merry party, and had the dixie going to make some tea. There was another dixie on, with two or three nice chickens that our fellows had got hold of—perhaps they had seen them wandering about homeless and adopted them.

Anyway, they found a good home in the stew-pot, and we were looking forward to a most cosy meal. As a sort of change from shelling by batteries in the ordinary way, we were being shelled from an armoured train, but were taking little notice of it, being busy with the tea and chickens.

The Germans were close enough to fling hand-bombs at us. They gave us lots of these little attentions, so that when I suddenly found myself blinded, and felt a sharp pain in my left hand, I thought they had made a lucky shot, or that something had exploded in the fire in the biscuit-tin.

For some time I did not know what had happened; then I was able to see, and on looking at my hand, I found it to be in a sorry mess, half the thumb and half a finger having been carried away.

I stayed and had some tea from the dixie, and my chums badly wanted me to wait for my share of the chickens; but I had no appetite for fowls just then. I made the best of things till darkness came, and under cover of it a couple of stretcher-bearers took me to the nearest dressing-station.

A horse ambulance unit in the British Army Medical Services Museum - Image: David Hawgood

I suffered intensely, and lockjaw set in, but the splendid medical staff and the nursing saved me, and I was put into a horse ambulance and packed off home. And here I am.

Chapter X – The British Victory at Neuve Chapelle

Sergeant Gilliam, Coldstream Guards.

[On the road from Béthune to Armentières, four miles to the north of La Bassée, is the little straggling frontier village of Neuve Chapelle, which first came into notice in October during the British advance to the north of La Bassée. At that time the village was held by the Germans, but on October 16th they were driven out by the British. As a result of the tremendous efforts of the Germans in trying to reach Calais we were not able to hold the village, which again was held by the enemy at the beginning of November. The British were driven back a short distance and for more than four months they remained near Neuve Chapelle; then, on March 10th they began an attack which ended in the village being retaken by us and held. The German Westphalian Army Corps in October and November had forced the British out of Neuve Chapelle, but in March these troops were routed and severely punished by part of Sir John French's "contemptible little army." What the battle meant and how it was fought is told by Sergeant Gilliam, 1st Battalion Coldstream Guards.]

THE battle of Neuve Chapelle began at half-past seven o'clock on the morning of March 10th, and ended at about half-past nine on the night of the 12th. Earlier on the morning of that famous day our battalion was ordered to stand to, as supports of the 1st Brigade. We were told to be ready to turn out at ten minutes' notice; and we *were* ready, for we were longing to have a settlement with the Germans, who had dug themselves in at Neuve Chapelle, and made themselves very comfortable and thought that no power on earth could drive them out. But we had a big surprise in store for them, and we sprung it on them like a thunderbolt when our massed guns roared soon after sunrise on that early day in March. Whatever advantages the Germans might have had at the beginning of the war we had been getting the better of them, and we were certain that we were now much superior to the enemy in every way. We knew that the British Army was becoming too much for them, and we were anxious to prove it that morning, when the biggest bombardment the world has ever known began, and along a tremendous front there came into action hundreds of the largest and the smallest guns that we had out in France.

I am sure that every man who was in at the beginning of this war, from Mons to the Marne and the Aisne, as I was, till I was invalided home wounded, will agree with me that there had been nothing like the British artillery fire at Neuve Chapelle. It was truly fearful. Something like five miles away, nearly five hundred British guns were bombarding the village, the batteries being on a front four or five miles in extent, so that there was only a few yards space between each gun. The result was that an immense wall of fire was seen where the artillery was in position, while the village itself was a target on which shells rained and made havoc. Nothing could withstand that awful cannonading—houses and buildings of every sort were shattered, and often enough a single shell was sufficient to destroy an entire house. When we got into the place at the end of the battle it looked as if some tremendous earthquake had upheaved it and thrown it down in a mass of wreckage. It was almost impossible to tell where the streets had been, and so enormous was the power of some of the shells that were fired and burst in the ground, that the very dead had been blown up from their resting-places in the churchyard, only to be re-buried by the falling walls around. The bombardment was bad enough for those who were out of it; for those who were in it the effect of the shell fire was paralysing. The Germans had had nothing like it, and more than one prisoner declared that it was not war, it was murder. We didn't quite see how they made that out; but it was near enough for the Germans, and we told them that we were only getting a bit of our own back for Mons. "And," we said, "this is only a taste of what's in store for you. It's nothing to what's coming!"

The roar of these massed guns was so deafening, and the noise of the exploding shells was so incessant, that we could not hear one another speak. The air was all of a quiver and you could see the heat in the atmosphere just as you see it when looking at the horizon in a tropical country, and as I saw it many times when we were in Egypt. The heat from the shells made the day for all the world like a hot summer day, and the fumes and flashes caused a strange mist that looked like rain, though the sun was shining.

The bombardment was grand and terrible beyond description; but there was one good thing about it, and that was that the Germans did not reply very often—they seemed numbed and stunned—and when they did, their fire was very slight and feeble, and so far as I could tell not one of their shells did any serious damage amongst the British forces.

For half-an-hour the British artillery bombarded the enemy's first line of trenches, and this fire to the Germans must have seemed as if hell had been let loose, because everything that was in the line of fire was blown away or levelled to the ground—walls, trees, buildings, sandbags, even the barbed wire entanglements were carried away by shell splinters and shrapnel bullets, though unfortunately some of the entanglements escaped injury, and became death-traps for a number of our fine fellows who were hurling themselves upon the Germans.

Perhaps I should explain, so that my story is quite clear, that Neuve Chapelle, or what is left of it, stands on perfectly flat ground, with plenty of enclosed gardens and orchards and some wooded country near. The Germans had dug themselves into very complete trenches, and had built some strong breastworks near the highroad into which they had put a large number of machine-guns. In houses and elsewhere these weapons had been planted, and in some places they fairly bristled. Our object was to rout the Germans out of their trenches and houses and barricades, and in view of the deadly nature of machine-guns and rifles the work was bound to be long and heavy and costly. How desperate the assault was has been shown by the losses of some of our splendid line battalions.

When the bombardment of the first line of trenches was over, the way had been paved for the infantry, who were lying in their trenches, not far from the village. They were waiting eagerly for the order to advance, and when it came, they sprang out of their trenches with such shouts that you might have thought a lot of lunatics had been let loose. They dashed forward, and almost before it was possible to realise what had happened they were in the nearest German trench.

Then it was, even so soon after the battle had opened, that we knew how destructive the fire of our guns had been, for when the trench was reached there was hardly a German left to tackle. Our shells had landed plump into the enemy, and the result was that the trench was full of dead and wounded Germans. The few survivors did not hesitate to explain that they felt as if they could shake hands with themselves and to marvel that any one of them had come out of such a fire alive.

Our men were full of joy at such an ending to their rush, full of satisfaction to feel that they were making such a fine score, then came one of those misunderstandings and mishaps which are part and parcel of a fight in which the artillery cannot always see what it is doing—our own poor fellows suddenly found themselves under the fire of our gunners, who had started bombarding the trench again under the impression that it was still held by the Germans.

Imagine, if you can, what it meant to be in a trench like that, at such a time—a long narrow pit which had been knocked about by shells and was crowded with débris and killed and wounded men, and then to be under our own shell-fire. With unerring aim the shells came into the trench, causing consternation, and yet a sort of grim humour. Above the cries of the wounded and the shouts of the men came the loud voices of the officers, saying, "What is our artillery thinking of? What are they doing?" And at the same time doing their dead best to get their men out of it and back to their own trenches.

The order was now given to retire to our old position, and at last the order was carried out, but still some of our men were puzzled to know what had taken place, and they shouted, "What's wrong?" "What's happened?" and so on, while there were many cries for help and water. It was soon seen that there had been a mistake, and the best was made of it, though that was not much consolation for poor chaps who had been badly mauled and knocked about by fire that was meant for the enemy.

Noon came round on that first day of the battle and the chief thing we knew was that what we thought was finished had not been done, and we had to start afresh; but there was no grumbling or whining. It was realised that there had been a mistake, and it was taken in the way of British soldiers. And we were well rewarded, for suddenly our artillery re-started. They knew by this time what had happened, and I think they must have felt pretty savage, judging from the nature of their fire. We could see the destructive effects of it from our trenches, and it was a wonderful yet awful sight to watch the Germans being blown out of their trenches into the air, some of the bodies being shot twenty or thirty feet high. I am not going to dwell on the havoc that was caused amongst men; but you can imagine how dismembered parts were scattered by such a continuous bursting of shells.

The bombardment stopped abruptly, and in the strange calm that followed it we went off again, in just the same high spirits as before. This time we were lucky; there was no mishap, things went well and right, and by half-past two we had the joy and pride of knowing that we had made ourselves masters of the first line of the German trenches.

This line was piled up with the German dead, and the first thing we did was to get to work to clear some of the bodies away, so as to make a bit of room for ourselves to stand, keeping at the same time well under cover in case the enemy tried to get their own back; but they had been too badly shaken, and nothing of this sort took place. The Germans believed that Neuve Chapelle could not be taken, as it was so strongly fortified, and we now had a chance of seeing how much ground they had for their belief. A particularly strong defence was the barbed wire entanglements, which had been made uncommonly thick and complicated. This was the reason why even our destructive fire did not cut through the entanglements and why some of our infantry suffered so heavily. The Liverpool Regiment lost terribly, as so many of the officers and men were caught in the wires and had no chance of escaping from the fire which the Germans mercilessly directed upon them. The Liverpools were caught between the cross-fire of two German maxims as they tried to cut through the barbed wire, just in front of the German trenches. It was real heroism on the part of the Liverpools and it was a ghastly sight to see the brave fellows being cut down like flies.

In our captured trench, which was nothing more than a huge grave, we began, when we had made ourselves secure, to snatch a few mouthfuls of food; but we had no sooner started on this pleasant task than down came the order to prepare to advance.

"That's right!" the men shouted. "The music's started again! Let's get at the German pigs!" Not very polite, perhaps, but in this war a good deal has been said on both sides about swine.

We sprang out of our trench and went full swing for the second trench—there were four trenches to storm and take before our object was accomplished. Very soon we were in amongst the Germans in the second trench, and it was a fine sight to see them being put through the mill.

Just in front of us, amongst the enemy, the shells from our own guns were bursting—a wonderful instance of the accuracy of modern artillery fire—and it was fascinating to see the shells sweeping every inch of the ground, and marvellous that human beings could exist in such a deadly area. Every now and then in would go one of the German parapets, and the almost inevitable accompaniment was the blowing into the air of limbs and mangled bodies. These things were not a laughing matter, yet often enough, as we watched a shell burst and cause havoc we laughed outright—

which shows how soon even the most dreadful of happenings are taken as matters of course.

Now came the order for us to assault and away the infantry went, right into the German trench, with such a rush and power that the enemy seemed to have no chance of standing up against the onslaught.

The men of the Leicestershire Regiment hurled themselves into the thick of the bloody fray, not once, nor twice, but five times in succession did they rush the Germans with the bayonet—and at the end of that tremendous onslaught they had not a single German prisoner! Never while a German lives who survived the charges of the Leicesters will he forget what happened in the trenches at Neuve Chapelle—and what the Leicesters did was done by the Irish Guards. No prisoners—and no man who has been through the war from the start will blame them, for he knows what the Germans have done to our own brave fellows, not in fair fight, but when they have been lying helpless on the roadside, especially in the retreat from Mons.

The long and thrilling day was ending, darkness was falling, and we pulled ourselves together and prepared for a lively night. We fully expected a counter attack, but no—it seemed to be the other way about, for on our left we had our famous Gurkhas and Sikhs, and they were getting ready for work.

It was quite dark, about half-past nine, when suddenly there was a shout in the German trenches, and as it rose in the night a pair of our star-lights burst, like bright, beautiful fireworks in the sky, and showed us what was happening. It was this—the Indians had moved swiftly and silently in the night, they had crept and crawled up to the German position, and before the enemy knew what was taking place the heavy curved knife, which is the Gurkha's pride, was at work, and that is a weapon against which the German soldier, especially when in the trenches, seems to have no chance whatever. It is almost impossible to get over your surprise at the way in which these brave little Indians cover the ground in attacking. They crawl out of their trenches at night, lie flat on their stomachs, with the rifle and the bayonet in the right hand, and wriggle over the ground like a snake and with amazing speed. Having reached the enemy's trenches they drop the rifle and bayonet and out come the knives—and woe betide the Germans that are within reach. The Gurkhas are born fighters, the love of battle is in their very blood, and they fight all the more readily and gladly because they believe that if they are slain they are sure to go to heaven. If a German makes a lunge at him, the Gurkha seizes the bayonet with the left hand and gets to work with the knife. The plucky little chaps get their hands badly ripped with the German bayonets, and many came into Neuve Chapelle with half their left hands off.

The Germans hate the sight of these Indians, and those who could do so escaped from the trench. They lost no time in going—they fled, and no wonder, for they had suffered terribly, not only from the Indians, but also from the Black Watch, who had been at them with the bayonets. The Highlanders took a large number of prisoners; but the German dead were everywhere, and the trench was packed with them—indeed, all the trenches at the end of the battle were filled with Germans.

During the 10th and 11th we made such good progress that we had taken three of the four trenches; then came the worst day of all, the 12th, for on that we were ordered to take the fourth trench which the Germans held. This was on the outskirts of the village and was strongly fortified. There was a strong blockhouse at the back of the trench which added greatly to the security of the position.

We were up and ready early—at half-past six—and as soon as day had broken the guns began their dreadful booming, and very solemn they sounded in the cold grey light, which is always so cheerless. The guns cleared the way again and did some excellent work in smashing away the wire entanglements and blowing up German works; then came the order to charge.

I was not in at the actual taking of this last trench, but I was lucky in being close enough to be able to see what was going on, and what I saw was some of the most furious fighting in the whole of the battle. The first charge was made with all the dash and courage of the infantry, who had already done so well. Our men rushed gallantly at the Germans; but so withering was the fire with which they were met and so hopeless seemed the obstacles that they were repulsed with heavy loss, and I know of nothing more heart-breaking to us who were watching than the sight of these soldiers being sacrificed and suffering as they did without, apparently, winning any success.

Again the artillery shelled the German position, then, across the ground which was littered with our dead and dying our brave fellows charged again. They sprang up from the shelter of their trenches, and with even greater fury than before threw themselves upon the enemy, only to be beaten back for the second time, by the cross fire of the machine-guns. In spite of all these losses and the awful odds against them our men kept their spirits up and vowed that they would still drive the enemy completely out of Neuve Chapelle, and get their own back for Mons and the rest of it, and so, while our artillery took up its tune again the men got a breather, and after a bombardment which lasted at least three-quarters of an hour there were shouts of "Now, boys, again! Let 'em have it!" And up the infantry sprang once more and dashed across the fatal ground. The men who were nearest to me were the 2nd Black Watch, and it did one's heart good to see the way the kilties swung towards the enemy's position. But it all seemed in vain, for at this point there was the blockhouse to be reckoned with. It was right in the centre and was a veritable little fortress which seemed a mass of flame and sent machine-gun and rifle bullets like hail. No troops could live or stand against such a fusillade, and so our men had to fall back even once more to the protection of the trenches.

By this time the position and danger of the blockhouse were known, and our artillery got the range of it, and that having been done, the end was merely a matter of time. A battery of British guns was trained on the blockhouse and the fire was so accurate that the fourth shell went through the left corner and the building was riddled with shrapnel and put out of action.

It was about this time that our fellows spotted an observation-post on the church in the village. As you know, churches and houses are objects that the British always avoid firing upon if they can, though the Germans have wantonly destroyed large numbers of both. There was the observation-post, plainly to be seen, and as the Germans were directing their artillery fire from it and the post was a danger and a nuisance to us and hindered our progress, a special effort was made to wipe it out. And the effort succeeded, for the British gunners got on it a "Little Harry," a shell that puts to shame even the Jack Johnsons and the Black Marias of the enemy. "Little Harry" settled the observation-post swiftly and finally, and then the fourth and last charge for Neuve Chapelle was made.

And what a charge it was! It was magnificent. Every bit of strength and courage that was left seemed to be put into it, and while the infantry dashed on with the bayonet and put the finish to the stubborn German resistance in the trenches and got the enemy fairly on the run, the Gurkhas and the famous Sikhs and Bengal Lancers hurled themselves on the flying regiments and cut them down with lance and sword.

"The infantry dashed on with the bayonet."

It was a wonderful swirl of fighting. This time the blockhouse was stormed by the 2nd Middlesex and the Royal Irish Rifles.

All at once the guns had finished, and with wild cheers the old "Die-Hards" and the Irishmen rushed to the German trench and would not be driven back. By about half-past three the blockhouse was taken, and then it was seen that it had been defended by no fewer than half-a-dozen machine-guns and two trench mortars, to say nothing of rifles. These weapons and thousands of rounds of ammunition were captured and the Germans who had not been killed were found hiding under cover as best they could and they were thankful to surrender.

While this splendid piece of work was being finished our Indians on the left were doing heavy execution. The Bengal Lancers were driving the fleeing enemy straight through the village, if that could be called a village which was now an almost shapeless mass of burning and smoking ruins. And spies and snipers had to be searched for in the shattered buildings, while we had to leave the captured trenches for two reasons, because they were filled with dead, and at any moment we might be blown out of them by mines which the Germans had laid. So we had to set to work, even while the fight was being finished, to construct new trenches, and we worked hard on these so as to make ourselves secure in case of a counter attack.

It was not long before we saw the victorious Indian cavalry returning. At about six o'clock we heard the thud of horses' hoofs, and looking up from the new trenches that we were making we saw the Bengal Lancers coming back from their pursuit and rout of the Germans. They had chased the enemy right through the village and into a big wood on the other side of Neuve Chapelle, and what they had done was shown by their reddened lances and the helmets and caps that were stuck on the steel. There were about six hundred of these fine horsemen and not one of them had less than two trophies on his lance, while I saw one of them with no fewer than eight skewered on, and he was smiling all over his dark handsome face. So were the rest of them—they were all delighted with the success that had crowned their work, and we cheered them mightily and laughed too, for somehow we couldn't help doing both.

Meanwhile we were being shelled from a spot which we could not locate for some time, then we learned that the firing came from a fort on the left of the village which was known as Port Arthur. We were in the direct line of fire from it, and our position became very uncomfortable. The Germans who were in Port Arthur were a plucky and stubborn lot, for they refused to surrender when they were asked to do so, and declared that they would not cave in either for British or French or Russians. That showed a fine and right spirit, but at last these chaps had to stop, because our gunners got two or three "Little Harrys" into Port Arthur, and it came tumbling down about the defenders' ears.

It was now dark, past nine o'clock, and it seemed that the enemy was a long time making up his mind to attack us; but at about twenty minutes past the hour they began firing with their artillery. The very first shell they sent came right into my two sections of trenches, and killed one man and wounded half-a-dozen of us, including myself. The poor fellow who was killed had his head completely taken off his shoulders. I helped to bandage the other five before I troubled about myself. Then I looked around again and found that the Germans were well into the night attack; but they never got within fifty yards of our trenches.

What happened after that I am not able to tell you. I was sent to the field ambulance to have my wounds dressed, then I learned that I had got two shrapnel bullets in me, one in the left thigh and one on the other side, to keep it company.

In the ambulance train I went to Béthune, then on to Boulogne, then, on a Sunday afternoon—the 14th of March— I landed at an English Channel port and once again had experience of the care and kindness of friends and nurses in the hospitals at home.

For the second time I had been sent home wounded from the front. I was proud enough when I felt that I had tried to do my duty in the glorious rearguard fighting after Mons and in the battles of the Marne and Aisne; but I was prouder still to know that I had shared in the victory of Neuve Chapelle, in which we got our own back, with a lot of interest, from some of the finest troops of Germany.

Australian soldiers depart for Europe from the Port of Melbourne - Image: Named Faces from the Past

Chapter XI – Sixteen Weeks of Fighting

Private B. Montgomery, Royal West Kent Regiment.

[Indomitable cheerfulness and consistent courage are two of the outstanding features of the conduct of the British soldier in the war, and these qualities are finely shown in this story of some of the doings of the 1st Battalion Queen's Own Royal West Kent Regiment, which has greatly distinguished itself and suffered heavily. Private Montgomery is a member of a fighting family, for he has a brother in the Royal Navy, two brothers in the Rifle Brigade, one in the Army Service Corps, and one in the Royal Army Medical Corps, so that there are six brothers serving their country in this time of urgent need.]

I DON'T know whether you have seen the picture of the retreat from Moscow, showing everybody going along in a drove, this, that, and the other way. You know it? Well, that wasn't a patch on some parts of the great retirement on Paris; but there was this enormous difference, that the retreat from Moscow was just that and nothing more, while our retirement was simply the beginning of what was to be a splendid victory.

It led up to the present tremendous fighting and this terrific trench work; and let me say that it is impossible for anybody who has not taken part in that trench warfare to realise what it means. Words and pictures will enable you to understand the life to some extent, but only by sharing in it will you fully realise its awful meaning.

But I'm not grumbling—I'm only stating a fact. Trench life is hard and dismal work, especially in a winter like this; but everything that it has been possible to do for the British soldier by the folk at home has been done.

Look at this—one of the new skin coats that have been served out to us. This is the way we wear it—yes, it certainly does smell, but it's goat-skin, and might have done with a bit more curing—and I can tell you that it takes a lot of even the wet and wind of the Low Countries to get through the fur and skin. These coats are splendid, and a perfect godsend.

I won't attempt to tell you about things exactly as they happened; I'll talk of them just as they come into my mind, so that you can understand what the Royal West Kents have done.

I can speak, I hope, as a fully-trained soldier, for I served eight years with the colours and two years in the Reserve before I was called up, and I did seven years abroad, in China, Singapore, and India; so I had got into the way of observing things that interest a soldier.

Well, one of my first and worst experiences was when at about ten-thirty at night the order for a general retirement was given, but through some mistake that order did not reach a sergeant and fourteen of the West Kents, of whom I was one, and it was not until just before four o'clock in the morning that we got the word, and began to try and pull ourselves out of it.

The Germans were then not more than eighty yards away from us, and our position was desperate. To make matters worse, the bridge by which we had to get across a neighbouring canal had been blown up, but as it happened the detonator on the overhead part of the bridge had not exploded, so that there was still a sort of communication across the water.

The bridge was full of wire entanglements and broken chains—a mass of metal wreckage—and the only way of crossing was to scramble along the ruins and crawl along what had been the iron parapet, which was only eight or nine inches wide. You will best understand what I mean if you imagine one of the iron bridges over the Thames destroyed, and that the principal thing left is the flat-topped iron side which you often see.

Under a terrible fire we made for the parapet and got on to it as best we could. I was the last man but one to get on to it. Just in front of me was Lance-corporal Gibson, and just behind me was Private Bailey.

With the Germans so near, so many of them, and keeping up such a heavy fire on us, you can imagine what it meant to crawl along a twisted parapet like that. The marvel is that a single one of us escaped, but a few of us did, which was no credit to the German marksmanship.

The bullets whizzed and whistled around us and very soon both the man in front of me and the man behind were struck.

The corporal was knocked straight over and disappeared. Bailey was shot through the instep, but he managed to hold on to the parapet, and to make a very singular request.

"Mont," he said, "come and take my boot off!"

I turned round and saw what had happened to him; but, of course, it wasn't possible to do what he asked, when it needed every bit of one's strength and skill to hang on to the parapet and keep crawling, so I cried back, "Never mind about taking your boot off—come on!"

It was no use saying anything; poor chap, he would insist on having his boot off, so I said, "For Heaven's sake get along, or we shall all get knocked over!" And with that I started to crawl again, and to get ahead as best I could.

The corporal, as I have said, had gone; he had been hit right between the shoulder-blades, and I just saw him roll over into the horrible barbed-wire entanglements.

What exactly happened to poor Bailey I don't know. I hadn't a chance of looking back, but I heard afterwards that both he and the corporal were found lying there, dead, with their faces spattered with blood.

At last, after what seemed like a miraculous escape, I got clear of the parapet, with a few more, and landed safely on the other side of the canal, looking for the West Kents; but it had been impossible to re-form any battalion, and regiments were walking about like flocks of sheep. Efforts were being made to re-form our own men, but at that time there was no chance of doing so.

It was the sight of these disorganised and wandering soldiers that brought to my mind the picture of the retreat from Moscow.

It was not until we reached Le Cateau that the handful of us rejoined the regiment, and so far as fighting went we merely changed from bad to worse.

At Le Cateau the West Kents held the second line of trenches, and the Yorkshire Light Infantry were in the first line, so that we were supporting them. We had the 121st and 122nd Batteries of the Royal Field Artillery in front of us—and no troops could wish for better gunners than the British.

We got into the trenches at about four-thirty on the morning of the 26th, and remained in them for something like twelve hours, and during that time we took part in what was probably the fiercest battle that had ever been fought up to that time, though there was worse to follow in the Ypres region. We were rather unlucky, as it happened, because we were forced to lie in the trenches and watch the other regiments and our artillery shelling the enemy without our being able to fire a shot, for we were so placed that we could not do anything effective against the enemy just then.

The Yorkshire Light Infantry retired, and then came the order for the West Kents to go. It was an order that needed the greatest care and courage to carry out, but it had been given, and, of course, the West Kents always do just what they are told to do. We did so now, with the result, I am proud to say, that we carried out Colonel Martyn's command to the letter.

"Don't get excited in any way," he said. "Just go off as if you were on battalion parade."

And we did, and the colonel showed us how to do it, for he walked off just as he might have walked off the barrack square, though all the time we were under heavy shell fire and our men were falling. We lost a fair number, but not many, considering the nature of the fire upon us.

We got as far as St. Quentin, which is a big town, trying to find out where our regiment had gone; but we got cold comfort, for a man came up and said: "It's no good going in there. The town's surrounded. The best thing you can do is to put down your arms and surrender."

We didn't relish the surrender suggestion, and we started to make inquiries. A sergeant who spoke French went up to a gendarme who was at the side of the railway station, and asked him if it was true that the town was surrounded.

The gendarme replied that he didn't know, but he believed the statement was true; anyway he advised us to remain where we were.

Not satisfied with that, about half a dozen of us went up to a French cavalry officer and put the question to him.

The cavalry officer, like the gendarme, said he didn't know, but told us that the best thing we could do was to go on to a place, which he named, about eight miles away, and off we went; but before we reached it we came across a cavalry division, and learned that it was not safe to go farther. Again we were advised to remain where we were, and we did for the time being.

It was not until later that we discovered what a narrow escape we had had, for three German cavalry divisions had been ordered to pursue the retiring troops hereabouts, but through a blunder the order had miscarried and the Uhlans did not follow us.

In such a serious business as this we had, of course, lost heavily, and we continued to lose. Major Buckle, D.S.O., one of the bravest men that ever stepped in a pair of shoes in the British Army, lost his life in attempting to distribute the West Kents. That is merely one of many instances of officers and men who were killed under fire.

Sometimes men were lost in the most extraordinary manner, especially owing to shell fire. At one time about six big shells burst, and in the wreckage caused by one of the explosions ten men were buried.

Men volunteered to go and try to dig these poor fellows out, but as fast as the volunteers got to work they, too, were shelled and buried, so that in the end about thirty men were buried—buried alive. It was useless to attempt to continue such a forlorn hope, and it was impossible to dig the men out, so they had to be left. It was hard to do this, but there was nothing else for it.

Bodies of men were lost, too, as prisoners, when overpowering numbers of Germans had to be met, or when the Germans rushed unarmed men and left them no alternative to capture. A doctor and twenty-five men of the West Kents who were acting as stretcher-bearers were taken. Very splendid work is done by the stretcher-bearers, who go to the trenches every night to collect the wounded, and bring them in to the hospitals. All sorts of buildings and places are used as hospitals, and in this case it was the cellar of a house in a village that was utilised. The men were not armed, as they were acting as members of the Royal Army Medical Corps, to render first aid.

Just about midnight the Germans broke through the line and surrounded the village, and rushed in and captured the stretcher-bearers, and took them off, no doubt thinking they had gallantly won a very fine prize.

I remember this particular occasion well, because on the following morning we were reinforced by some of the native Bhopal Infantry, from India, and that took me back to the time I spent in that country. Little did I think in those days, when we were associated so much with the troops of the Indian Army, that the day would come when, in the heart of winter, we and the Indians would be fighting side by side in the awful Low Countries.

I got used to the heat of the day and the cold of the night in India, but it wasn't easy to become accustomed to the sweltering heat of the earlier days of the war, or the bitter cold of the winter.

One day, not long before I came home, we had six miles to do, after a very heavy fall of snow. We ploughed through the snow in the daytime, and at night we travelled in the transport, but what with the snow by day and the bitter freezing by night, we were fourteen hours covering that short distance—which works out at something under half a mile an hour. And that was the roundabout way we had to go to get at some enemy trenches which were only about fifty yards away from us. But, in spite of this terrific weather, we had only one or two cases of frost-bite.

A change on trench work and actual fighting came with my being told off as an ammunition carrier. There are two ammunition carriers to each company, and our duty was to keep the firing line well supplied with ammunition. This we fetched from the pack-mules, which were some distance away, and we took it to the men in the firing line in bandoliers, which we filled from the boxes carried by the mules. It was lively work, especially when the mules turned awkward and the firing was hot; but we got through it all right—Lance-Corporal Tweedale and myself.

One night, when the shell and rifle fire was very heavy, we went up to the firing line with ammunition, which was badly wanted, and we had such a hot time of it that the officer in charge advised us to remain for a couple of hours, till the firing slackened or ceased; but we had a feeling that it would be more comfortable in the rear, and as the matter rested with us we started off to get back.

This was one of the most uncomfortable bits of journeying I ever undertook, for in order to shelter from the fire of the Germans, which threatened every second to kill us, we had to crawl along a ditch for fully three-quarters of a mile. We crawled along in the darkness, with the bullets whizzing and shells bursting; but we lay low, and at last got out of it and landed back at the rear, which was certainly more agreeable than being in the very thick of the firing line.

I am proud to be one of the Royal West Kents, because they have done so well in this great war. "Give 'em a job and they'll do it," a general said of us, just after Le Cateau. One day another general said, "What regiment is that coming out of the trenches?" The answer was, "The Royal West Kent, sir," and the general promptly said, "For Heaven's sake give them a rest—they've earned it!" But we hadn't gone more than two hundred yards when a staff officer told us to get into position in a field and dig ourselves in—and we were the last out of action that day.

At another time, when we had been hard at it, a general said: "Come on, West Kents! In another half-hour you'll be in your billets." And we went on, for that sounded very cheerful; but, instead of going into billets, we had half-an-hour's rest for a drop of tea—then we went on outpost duty for the night, and woke in the morning in a big scrap.

I am mentioning these things just to show how unexpectedly disappointments came at times; but we soon got into the way of taking these set-backs as part of the day's work.

When the winter advanced, the strain became uncommonly severe, but we were able to bear it owing to the first-rate system of relief we had—a relief which gave us as much change as possible on the confinement and hardship of the actual trenches.

Some very strange things happened in the trenches, and none were stranger than those cases of men being in them for long periods under heavy fire and escaping scot free, to be succeeded by others who lost their lives almost as soon as they got into their places.

There was one youngster—he could not have been more than seventeen or eighteen—who had been in France only about a fortnight. He was having his second day in the trenches, and, like a good many more who are new to the business, he was curious to see what was going on. This was particularly dangerous, as the Germans were only sixty yards away, and any seen movement on the part of our men brought instant fire.

The officer kept telling the youngster to keep down, and more than once he pulled him down; but the lad seemed fascinated by the port-hole of the trench—the loop-hole, it is generally called—and he looked through it again; once too often, for a German marksman must have spotted him. Anyway, a bullet came through the port-hole and struck the lad just under the eye, went through his brain, and killed him on the spot.

I will give you another curious instance, that of Sergeant Sharpe. It was his turn to be in reserve, but he had volunteered to go up to the trenches, to look round. He had scarcely had time to put his feet in them before a shot came and struck him between the eyes, killing him instantly.

I specially remember the sad case of the inquisitive youngster, because it happened on the very day I was wounded, and that was December 16. I was in a trench, sitting over a coke fire in a biscuit tin, when a bullet struck me on the chin—here's the scar—then went to the back of the trench, where it struck a fellow on the head, without seriously hurting him, and came back to me, hitting me just over the right eye, but not doing any serious mischief. After that I was sent into hospital, and later on came home.

On the way back I came across two very singular cases. One was that of a man who had had his arm amputated only a fortnight previously, and he was not used to it. He used to turn round and say, "I keep putting up my hand to scratch the back of it—and the hand isn't there!"

I saw another poor fellow—quite a youngster—who was being carried on a stretcher to the train. Both his legs had been blown off by a shell. I was right alongside when he said, "For Heaven's sake cover up my feet—they're cold!" He lived for about half an hour after that, but never reached the train.

There is one thing I would like to say in finishing, and that is to thank our own flesh and blood for what they have done for us. I'm sure there never can have been a war in which so much has been done in the way of sending presents like cigarettes and tobacco; but I think that too much has been sent at one time, and that friends would do well to keep some of the good gifts back a bit. They will all be wanted later on.

Printed in Poland
by Amazon Fulfillment
Poland Sp. z o.o., Wrocław